Secrets to Entrepreneurial Success

...Giving Entrepreneurs an Edge, Learned from Years in the Entrepreneurial Trenches

By
Lonnie L. Sciambi
"The Entrepreneur's Yoda"

Copyright © 2012 Lonnie L. Sciambi
All rights reserved.
ISBN-13: 978-0615693651 (Small Business Force, LLC)
ISBN-10: 0615693652

DEDICATION

This book is dedicated to my longstanding partner, who has been there with me through every entrepreneurial moment, alongside every risk, sharing those heady upside times (and, unfortunately, those few downside ones), never failing to be my sounding board, my encouragement and, when necessary, my strongest critic - my wife, Helen, the love of my life.

ACKNOWLEDGEMENTS

This book would not have seen the light of day without the encouragement, actually harassment, from my good friend and former partner, Wayne Nystrom, who was convinced that I had the makings of a book nearly a year before I was.

Additionally, I want to thank the many companies I have been involved with, as founder, CEO and advisor, for providing me the opportunity to work with them, giving me the basis for the subject matter and examples, both good and bad, that I use throughout the book. Hopefully, my advice put you on the path for leveraging your positives and fixing your negatives.

Finally, I want to acknowledge all entrepreneurs. You are today's pioneers, taking your virtual covered wagons into uncharted territories, chasing your dreams in the hopes of creating something that doesn't exist today and along the way creating a better life for you and your family and maybe even the world around you. I stand solidly with you.

Table of Contents

Introduction - "Now All We Have to Do is Build It and Fly It..."..13

Chapter 1 - All Startups Are Not Created Equal.............19

"What Are the Key Traits for Entrepreneurial Success?"..20

"You Must Unlearn What You Have Learned!"................21

"Don't Be Fooled by the 'Big Numbers' Game!" 24

"Prove It! Do Whatever You Can to Get Your First Customer...As Early As Possible!" 26

"Another Startup Myth – 'If I Build It, They Will Come!'" 27

"100% of Zero is Still Zero!"..29

"The Market Learning about Your Start-up Can Be Like Someone Trying to Find You in Times Square on New Year's Eve!" 31

"They Just Don't Get It!" 33

"Instead of Filing That Patent, Why Not Just Post Your Product Design on a Billboard on the NJ Turnpike!" 35

"If Failure is Not an Option...Then Neither is Success!" ..38

"Want to Take on Long Odds? Try Introducing a New Product That's 'Better' Than an Established Product!" 40

"Entrepreneurs Need to Learn How to Say 'No!'" 42

"You Probably Have Not Discovered Fire! But If You Have, Your Work Has Just Begun!" 44

"Not All Startups Can Succeed, or... Even Passion and Hard Work Won't Overcome A Bad Business Concept!" 47

"It's Lonely at the Top... Guidance for the Early Stage CEO" 51

Chapter 2 – Don't Just Have a Clue. Have a Strategy...and a Plan!..55

"If Your Business Doesn't Have a Plan, You May Soon Not Have a Business!" 56

"Without Objectives, There Can Be No Real Strategies and without Real Strategies There Can Be No Long-Term Success!" 59

"Ready, Fire, Aim! How Premature Execution Dooms a Good Plan." 62

"Never Waste a Time at Bat! Good Advice in Baseball, Even Better in Small Business!" 65

"Are You Building a Business That's '80 Miles Wide and An Inch Deep?'" 68

"Being Small May Well be Your Biggest Asset!" 71

"Adapt or Die! React to Market Changes before They Force Change on You." 74

"And What Happens to the Business If You Get Hit by a Bus?" 78

Chapter 3 – There's Safety in Numbers! Look for Partners and Advisors..81

"Partner Your Way to Success" 82

"Free Advice Is Usually Worth What You Pay For It!" 84

"'Tap the Gray Hair!' – Creating and Using an Advisory Board/Board of Directors" 86

"Is Your Nose Pressed Right Up Against a Tree as You Are Trying to See the Forest?" 90

"Advisor, Mentor, Coach. No Matter What They're Called, Results Are All That Matter!" 94

Chapter 4 – It All Starts with Marketing......................97

"Know Your Battlefield, Pick Your Battles" 98

"If It Ain't Generating Qualified Leads, Don't Do It!" 101

"'First Perceptions' Are Critical... Your Image Can Drive Market Success!" 103

"Being In A Competitive Market Ain't Bad News!" 106

"With Limited Resources, Would You Invest in Technology or Marketing?" 109

"Want to Sell More Customers? Make It About Them!" 111

"'Happy Birthday from ABC Ford' – Good Plan, Crummy Execution" 113

Chapter 5 – It Ends with Sales. Without Sales, There is No Business!...117

"Do You Sleep with Your Sales Forecast Under Your Pillow?" 118

"Do You Lead with Price…Leaving Money on the Table and Losing Potential Customers in the Process?" 121

"Are the Results of Your Chasing 'Big Wins' Just a Closet Full of Pastel-Colored Dresses?" 124

"Is Your Sales and Marketing Strategy Simply SATW?" 127

Chapter 6 – Love and Support Your Customer!..................131

"Are You Making It Easy for Customers to Do Business With You?" 132

"In a Small Business, Building a Customer Base is the Lifeblood of Success…and Everybody Has a Role, Including the Customer!" 134

"A Good Customer Relationship is Built on Appreciation and Begins with 'Thank You!'" 138

"Customer Service…The Choice for Growth!" 140

Chapter 7 – Building a Successful Organization is about the Culture You Create and How You Treat Employees..143

"The Culture You Create Is the Soul of Your Enterprise!" 144

"Celebrate Small Victories!" 148

"Hiring the Right People…and Holding them Accountable Is Critical to Growing Your Business!" 150

"People - Engaging and Motivating Them Is One of the Keys to Small Business Success!" 153

"Your Employees Will Treat Your Customers The Way They Themselves Are Treated." 156

"Do You Allow Your Employees to Fail?" 159

Chapter 8 – Finance – It's Way More Than "Bean Counting;" Way More Than Raising Capital 161

"To the Entrepreneur, Cash is Almost as Important as Breathing (But Only a Close Second)" 162

"To the Entrepreneur, Cash is Almost as Important as Breathing (But Only a Close Second)" - Part II 165

"Is The Financial System for Your Small Business Just a 'Virtual Cigar Box?'" 168

"Numbers Are Important. Which Ones Do You Use to Manage Your Small Business?" 172

"Are You Using the Lack of Capital As An Excuse?" 174

"6 Key Things Entrepreneurs Should Consider Before Seeking Outside Investment." 177

"Is Your Business Plan Written for Your Prospective Investor…or More Likely, Your Prospective Customer?" 181

Chapter 9 – Operations - Where the Rubber Meets the Road 185

"Are You The Major Bottleneck in Your Own Company?" 186

"To Increase Success, Entrepreneurs Should Use Industry Best Practices as Processes to Improve On!" 189

"R-E-S-P-E-C-T– Don't Forget Your Vendor Is A Business Owner Too! Make The Vendor A Partner Instead of Just A Supplier." 191

"'Win, Win' Should be an Objective in Every Business Relationship!" 194

"Are You Allowing Employees, Suppliers or Customers to Hold You Hostage?" 197

Chapter 10 – Starting the Business is the Easy Part; Growing It is Where the Greatest Challenges Are 201

"The Gerbil Syndrome" 202

"You Can't Be a 'One Ball Juggler' and Be a Successful Entrepreneur" 204

"In a Small Business, There Are No Absolutes. Everything is Relative. What Works, is What Works for You!" 207

"Little Failures Are Often More Important to Entrepreneurs Than Big Successes. You Learn More!"... 210

"Change Can Protect You From Small Business Failure!" 213

"You Know, You Are Allowed to Have Fun in Business!" 216

"To Achieve Entrepreneurial Success, You Can Never Know Too Much!" 219

"The Extra Step is Often the Difference between Real Entrepreneurial Success and Just Getting By." 222

"Be Careful What You Wish For…Success Always Comes at a Price!" 225

Chapter 11 – What's Your End Game? And Beyond? 229

"What's Your "End Game?" Do You Really Have One? Or Need One?" 230

"'Take This Exit' – Selling Your Business: The Entrepreneur's Potential End Game" - Stage I – The Decision to Sell 232

"'Take This Exit' – Selling Your Business: The Entrepreneur's Potential End Game" - Stage II – The Plan 238

"'Take This Exit' – Selling Your Business: The Entrepreneur's Potential End Game" - Stage III – The Approach 246

"'Take This Exit' – Selling Your Business: The Entrepreneur's Potential End Game" - Stage IV – The Deal 254

About the Author **265**

Introduction - "Now All We Have to Do is Build It and Fly It..."

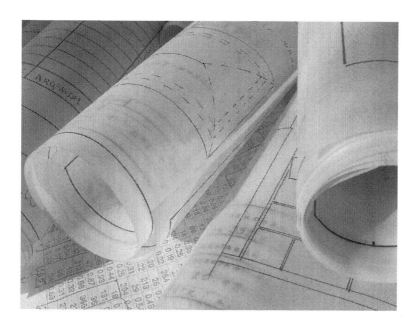

Several years back, after doing a series of turnarounds, I returned to advising entrepreneurial businesses. For those of you who know me, you know that I operate with a certain degree of levity and whimsy. So along that line, I branded myself "The Entrepreneur's Yoda," based on the depth of my experience and the wealth of wisdom and advice I wanted to share to help entrepreneurs and small business owners succeed (to say nothing of my advancing years and well-earned "gray hairs").

As part of that sharing, I created a blog. I've had a great deal fun and gotten a lot of satisfaction from both the branding and the blog. This book is compilation of many of my blog posts. They are all based on real-life experiences that I had as an entrepreneur, investment banker, turnaround specialist, CEO of small businesses, both public and private, and consultant/advisor to a myriad of companies of varying sizes across multiple markets.

The quote, that introduces the book, is one of my favorites. It comes from set of cartoon slides (hey, remember, Yoda is old and we used slides before PowerPoint was even a glimmer in Bill Gates eyes) I used to use as part of workshop presentations and speeches I did. It depicts Orville and Wilbur Wright looking over the plans for the airplane, with Orville saying to Wilbur, "now all we have to do is build it and fly it!" I think this kind of summarizes how a lot of would-be entrepreneurs start out. They have an idea and well, it's just a matter of creating the product, and the market beating a path to their door to gain success...and riches beyond their wildest imagination! And as most of you have already found out...it doesn't work that way.

This book is aimed, specifically, to help entrepreneurs get their business to "the next level," whether that level be moving beyond startup or shaking up a stagnant business to get it back on a growth cycle. Or exit after years of growing your business.

I put it together because there didn't seem to be anything out there that just helped entrepreneurs, whether with some straightforward advice or to just help them solve problems without a lot of fanfare. It seemed like everything that was around that was deemed to help an entrepreneur was either written by someone who sounded like they were giving a seminar to second year "B school" students, a consultant presenting a report to a Fortune 500 company or a "successful" entrepreneur, who just happened to have been at the right place at the right time during the internet bubble

Introduction

and sold his company for a jillion dollars, without really having to work very hard to get there. Long on words, short on usable solutions.

I thought something was needed that was direct, practical and useful, that came from real-world experience - a lot of success...and a lot of failure (because it is truly through failure that we learn our most important lessons). And I've surely had both!

Some of my advice might make you laugh; some of it you might disagree with. But all of it will make you think. Hopefully, each "secret" unlocks an idea or a concept that might in some way, contribute to your success as an entrepreneur.

The book is organized along critical functions of the continuum of entrepreneurship from startup through exit with the following critical "secrets":

- Chapter 1 – **"All Startups Are Not Created Equal!"** - Provides guidance, "how-to" approaches and pitfalls to avoid, assisting those of you who are either thinking about starting up a new business, are in the early stages of your small business roll-out, or have already launched and have some early revenue and customers. It will help keep you focused on what's important for early success.

- Chapter 2 – **"Don't Just Have a Clue. Have a Strategy...and a Plan!** - Uniquely describes the importance of setting goals and objectives, creating strategies and tactics, to achieve them and developing practical, workable plans to execute them in a timely manner. Additionally, we'll talk about the ongoing need stay prepared and vigilant, especially at it relates to the markets you serve and any critical changes they are undergoing.

- Chapter 3 – "There's Safety in Numbers! Look for Partners and Advisors." - What you learn real early in the entrepreneurial game is that "going it alone," is a very limiting strategy. This chapter's "secrets" show how the use of "outside" organizations and people can help better leverage the precious resources you have within your small business at various growth stages. How partners can help expand capabilities and markets while offsetting risk. How advisors can assist you in avoiding pitfalls and navigate early stage and ongoing growth by virtue of their own similar experiences.

- Chapter 4 – "It All Starts with Marketing…" - Helps you understand the importance of marketing, and how it drives everything from market understanding, including target markets and competition to generating qualified leads. It will show you how to not only develop more effective marketing plans, but how those marketing plans affect and are affected by other functions within your company.

- Chapter 5 – "It Ends with Sales. Without Sales, There is No Business!" – Gives you some critical guidance about what's important (and what's not) in closing more business. It shows you how to more effectively work specific situations to your advantage as a small business to drive revenue.

- Chapter 6 - "Love and Support Your Customer!" - Shows you why it's essential to your success to "love" your customer and some really simple, straightforward ways to make them love you back. And it describes the

Introduction

"dirty little secret" of revenue generation – customer service!

- Chapter 7 - **"Building a Successful Organization is About How the Culture You Create and How You Treat Employees."** – Once you've hired your first employee, you start to build an organization. Here, the importance of a creating a culture built on founder values and how to make employees, and therefore the company, thrive in that environment is addressed. Additionally, we'll provide "secrets" to how to keep those two elements (employee growth and company success) linked.

- Chapter 8 – **"Finance – It's Way More Than 'Bean Counting;' Way More Than Raising Capital!"** - Demonstrates how to not only how better generate and manage your cash but how to know what numbers to track and why. Additionally, we'll show you how to prepare for and develop fundable plans for raising necessary growth capital.

- Chapter 9 – **"Operations – Where the Rubber Meets the Road!"** – Provides 'secrets" for helping you to better run your day-to-day operations and processes, including better employee and vendor interactions. We'll also address how to create, negotiate and manage better external business relationships that can assist your growth.

- Chapter 10 – **"Starting the Business is the Easy Part; Growing It is Where the Greatest Challenges Are."** - Guides you through ways to get your business on a solid growth track (and know why). It also provides some critical guidance on how to continue to grow top and bottom line, over time, while avoiding the pitfalls that many entrepreneurial companies fall into trying to grow.

- Chapter 11 – "What's Your End Game? And Beyond? - And finally, we'll give you essential guidance to help you to develop an "end game" strategy and if exit is part of that, take you through a step-by-step process to assist you to, ultimately, monetize all of your efforts.

A few last words of warning.

Remember that these were individual blog posts written over several years, so there are some positions, thoughts and concepts that recur, periodically. Know that if that is the case they ARE important. So don't be ragging on me about some repetitive stuff. Look at it as Yoda's way of making a point (and hiding the fact that "gray hairs" do repeat themselves, periodically).

I hope you enjoy reading each segment as much as I enjoyed writing each of them. And along the way I hope, in some small way, I can contribute to your growth and success as an entrepreneur. And once you learn the "secrets," use them, improve on them and, most of all, pass them on. That's how real growth happens. We pay it forward! And as I signed every blog post:

Master Yoda knows these things. His job it is. May success be with you!

Lonnie L. Sciambi
"The Entrepreneur's Yoda"
September 2012

Chapter 1 - All Startups Are Not Created Equal

"What Are the Key Traits for Entrepreneurial Success?"

I don't think there is a question that people ask more. At a talk before several hundred would-be entrepreneurs this past weekend, I was asked it again. So I thought this would be a good place to provide the answer I give time and time again. It's so simple, yet so powerful. While nothing can absolutely ensure success, there are two key traits that dramatically increase the odds for success for an entrepreneur:

- An unbridled passion for a business concept that fills a specific market need and one that you can deliver a product or service that meets that need.

- Near-religious zeal for managing your cash, with cash generation as your primary focus at all times.

Only two, but the most powerful of any you can bring to your endeavor. And the ones that will most contribute to your ultimate success. If you can achieve them, you can succeed!

"You Must Unlearn What You Have Learned!"

Words from the original Yoda that ring true whether seeking to become a successful Jedi warrior or a business warrior. We are products of our environment, our life and work experiences. Sometimes those experiences are of great help in starting and running a small business. Sometimes, not so. But in any case, you need to understand that and determine the habits or attitudes that may be roadblocks to your success as an entrepreneur.

Just like on a personal level, how you grew up, family size, socio-economic situation, etc., drive a lot of how you act and think; on a professional level, where you have worked (company and relative size) and for whom (the culture and environment) drive a lot of your professional behavior and thinking.

For example, growing up as an only child, the concept of sharing, might need to be learned, as opposed to in a large family, where it exists as a matter of course. If you grew up in an upper-scale environment, you might have a sense of privilege and never faced real adversity. On the other hand, growing up lower-middle class, you may have been surrounded by it

When it comes to business, the same things holds true.

If you came from a big company, you had the security of knowing that your paycheck would be there every 15th and 30th of the month. Administrative things like travel arrangements or ordering supplies simply "got done" by somebody. Most typically, you learned a lot about mind-numbing process and procedures that ensured that everybody's a***s were covered and it was almost impossible to get any kind of decision made without multi-layers of committees and decision-makers.

From this platform, becoming an entrepreneur will be like having a bucket of ice cold water dumped on your head.

As the owner, as least until the business gets traction, regular paychecks may be non-existent. Travel arrangements won't get made...unless you do them. Supplies won't simply be in the closet down the hall (unless, of course, you bought them and put them there). All heavy-duty process will do is slow down progress. And finally, all major decisions get done solely from the person staring back at you in the mirror...and that's the only a** that matters!

If you enter into an entrepreneurial environment without understanding and accepting these "facts of life," you'll make yourself crazy and soon find yourself out of business.

On the other hand, if the security truly doesn't matter as much as the freedom you have as an entrepreneur; and you don't mind having to do things for yourself that others have done for you for years (and you might even think you could do better), and if the mind-numbing processes and glacier-like decision cycles have been frustrating you to tears, then maybe, just maybe, you're ready to change. Then maybe you're ready for the challenges the entrepreneurial life can bring...and the potential success that it can promise.

All Startups Are Not Created Equal

For entrepreneurial success, learn what you need. Unlearn what you don't!

"Don't Be Fooled by the 'Big Numbers' Game!"

I can't tell you how many business plans I've reviewed that were built on the premise that the market for the product or service of the business was simply astronomical and that all that was necessary was simply capturing a miniscule percentage of that market. This is a great Excel exercise, but usually quite short of reality.

Just because you have market of x thousands (or millions) of potential customers means nothing unless you can show that you have realistic strategies and plans that specifically identify what their need is for your product or service, (typically that brings down the potential customer numbers pretty dramatically) and can convert them from prospects to customers. That is, how do you plan on capturing that miniscule market percentage?

The corollary caution to this mistake is when a company has a product or service that has potential application in both the corporate and consumer markets. While the corporate market will allow significantly higher price points, a more feature-rich product and a tighter focus, the numbers for "potential" for the consumer market seems just too good to pass up. And the company either focuses totally on the consumer market, or worse, on both.

All Startups Are Not Created Equal

What is missed under this scenario is that for any sales plan to succeed it has to identify potential customers, reach them to let them know who you are, learn why your product or service is good for them and then to convert them to customers. The cost to market a product or service to the consumer market invariably requires enormously deep pockets to create this awareness and interest, because it is so diffused and needs to be sustained to be effective.

Now, I'm not saying to avoid the markets where the potential is so huge, or to avoid the consumer market. Only to understand that to attack a large market requires a solid plan to capture share. The bigger the potential market, the more detailed the plan and the more capital required to sustain it.

So, don't focus on how big the market is, but how do you capture a rational share of it and what resources you need to effectively do that.

"Prove It! Do Whatever You Can to Get Your First Customer...As Early As Possible!"

While it may seem obvious, you can't spend enough early time getting customers. More than just a good business plan, you need real-live customers as early as possible to take your concept or product to the reality stage.

Get people using it, even if you have to give the early ones away or charge a fraction of your desired selling price. If your product is good, you'll have real customers to confirm that with prospects. If it still needs work, you've got real feedback to help you tweak it toward success.

"Another Startup Myth – 'If I Build It, They Will Come!'"

There are countless examples, especially in the technology space, where the entrepreneur is so passionate in his/her belief in the business concept that they expend all available resources to continue to optimize the product/service that underpins the business concept. They operate under the mistaken notion that the product/service is so good that it will be intuitively obvious for potential customers to gravitate to it and buy it. And unlike the movie, "Field of Dreams," just because you build it, they not only won't come...*they won't even know you exist!*

This brings us to today's Entrepreneur's Yoda words of wisdom – "**Good marketing beats good technology every single time!**" In essence, spend as much time (and resources), or more, creating and executing your marketing plans as you do creating and executing your product development plans. To further emphasize this point, is a corollary, formed by one of my most respected business partners – "**Nobody ever bought a product or service that they didn't know about!**"

The meaning here is clear. Getting your product or service ready for market is but one part of the battle. The critical elements for success are what you do to make potential customers aware of your product and then what you do to turn them into actual, cash-paying customers. With both time and cash resources typically in short supply for a small business, it's better to develop a basic product and maximize your marketing and sales efforts than to develop the ultimate product with no resources left to market it.

If most of the skills your small business possesses are product development as opposed to sales and marketing, rather than hire someone, find a partner (a non-competitor), who operates in your target market to help you roll out your product. Whether that be a larger company with already existent sales channels or a smaller company who operates with a complementary product or some combination. (More on strategic partnerships in another chapter.)

Getting awareness for your product and being able to create interest in it once you do may actually be more important than the product itself.

All Startups Are Not Created Equal

"100% of Zero is Still Zero!"

In the early growth stages of your company, don't be overly concerned with the percentage of equity you retain. By either setting too high a valuation and/or making sure you keep controlling interest, you might do so at the detriment of being able to get the right staff and early capital you need to get the business growing.

The name of the game is how much the equity is worth, not how much you have. With each dilution, should come more value. If you're raising capital, no matter where you think your valuation should be, your investors (and the market) will tell you what it is. Then you need to decide if your new ownership percentage, with that investment, is worth the same or more than it would be, pre-investment.

Establish an option program as soon as possible after establishing the business, if not at the outset. If possible, make all employees eligible to become "owners" through the grant of options. It can help you conserve cash by keeping early salaries below market and really help you with employees during "lean times." Use options as incentives. And remember options can help reinforce employee retention because they have to "be present to win." That is, with most option programs, typically, there is a vesting period. And if they leave with vested options, they still are not technically shareholders until they exercise those options.

Make your equity work for you. It does you no good to own 100% of something that is not increasing in value. Create value through either outside investment (and how you leverage that capital) or inside ownership (where each individual "owner" is striving to increase the value of his/her stake each day), or both!

"The Market Learning about Your Start-up Can Be Like Someone Trying to Find You in Times Square on New Year's Eve!"

Picture yourself in Times Square on New Year's Eve and wanting a group of friends to find you. There are a million people all around you. You need to stand out, so you can be easily spotted. What would you do? Wear a red hat? Then you've narrowed yourself down to the group of, perhaps, ten thousand wearing a red hat. Maybe hold up a sign? Maybe you're down to a thousand of you with red hats and signs. You get the picture.

Never in history has there been so much market "noise," with people bombarded with messages and information.

On a comparable note, for the entrepreneur, how does the market learn about your start-up? How does your message get through the noise? How does it stand out in the crowd?

That's your challenge and, unfortunately, there's no easy or right answer.

But, the best place to start is to tighten your focus. In the Times Square metaphor that means telling folks to look for you on the west side of Broadway, and more specifically, on the corner of West 44th and Broadway. Now, you're among maybe a thousand folks, but remember you're wearing your red hat and carrying a sign. Now, it's you and ten other folks (with red hats and signs). Much easier task for your friends.

And for your startup, a much easier task for folks to learn about it if you continue to tighten your focus to the target market that is most in need of your small business' product or service to solve a problem or meet a need they have. With limited resources, you *can't* do a "Times Square" marketing campaign. You need a "44th and Broadway, Red Hat and Sign" strategy instead. It makes every element of your plan easier to implement because it has a specific target. Whether that be using social media or more traditional marketing, or both.

Get focused, let your message get through!

All Startups Are Not Created Equal

"They Just Don't Get It!"

Having spent most of my career around technology, I have always been fascinated by the brilliance, intensity and passion of the entrepreneurs, engineers and scientists in that space. I have been equally taken aback by their, often, total lack of understanding or empathy with their prospective customer or user. How often have I heard the phrase "they just don't get it," either directly or through intimation?

And maybe they never will...if you make it the target audience's responsibility to "get it." People will not buy something they can't understand. And it's the responsibility of the designer, developer, sales person or small business owner to make sure their audience "gets it."

I just had another reaffirmation of this with a client for whom I'm helping put a business plan together. I try to get young companies to own the plan by acting during the entire plan development process as "the prospective audience." This forces the entrepreneur to describe his/her business model in ways my average brain (and, in turn, the average brain of the prospective audience) will understand. After I asked my client for about the tenth iteration of the basic business model description, in frustration he said, "You just don't get it." He was really the one that didn't get it. He could not put his business model into simple, concise terms that his prospective audience would understand and want to partner with or invest in.

How often have you been faced with a similar situation? An obvious opportunity that you could not seem to capitalize on because the prospective customer was just "too dense." Or was it that he wasn't "in your head," knowing what you know. He was thinking in terms of his own business, his own needs and requirements...just the way he should be. And the way you should be!

Having a user focus in everything you do in your small business is essential for any degree of success. This is the basis of "the elevator pitch" everyone tells you that you need (and you do, and not just for pitching investors). And it works whether you're explaining what your business or your product does to a prospective customer, employee, investor, your significant other, or...even one of your kids.

To reach your audience you have to help them "get it," by portraying your business concept in simple, concise terms that make them understand and want to know more. With as little techno-babble and industry-specific phrases as possible. And find a way (in each situation) to relate what you do to something relevant to their particular situation. Audience empathy!

Think about the sentence or two that you use, today, to depict your business or product (and if it takes more than that it's too complicated). Could you use it to tell your aging Aunt Letitia what you do? If you can't, then you need to modify your message. Otherwise, nobody will "get it!"

"Instead of Filing That Patent, Why Not Just Post Your Product Design on a Billboard on the NJ Turnpike!"

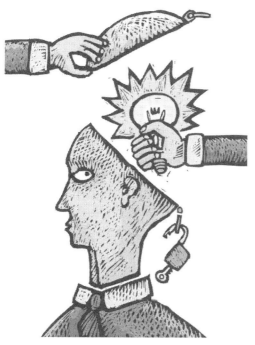

While patents, ostensibly, provide the foundation for and the protection of intellectual property, without a strategy and plan to implement the underlying invention and the capital to defend it, you might just as well put your product design on a billboard on the NJ Turnpike. And worse, there are, literally, tens of thousands of patents like that.

Filing a patent is often viewed as a critical step for an entrepreneur. But what it represents, in terms of protection of their "invention," is deceptive. If it is approved, it means that it is illegal for anyone to copy or use the design at its foundation, but without a practical implementation of that design, it is simply a novel idea; an idea that is most vulnerable.

When a patent is filed and it is approved, that product design is now in the **public domain**. By law, it is available to ANYONE who accesses it. ANYONE can view read, copy it, even build the product upon which it is based. (Hence, my NJ Turnpike metaphor). You are making "the family jewels" available to potentially larger, better funded competitors, who might take your concept and enhance it, take it in another direction or simply implement it EXACTLY as you have designed it. And then dare you to sue them! And, it's up to the patent holder to defend what is, obviously, a "patently" illegal act.

Further, and perhaps most important, even if it has a practical implementation, without the money to defend it or a strategy and plan to capitalize on it and build market share, your idea is susceptible for anybody to steal!

Further, many fledgling entrepreneurs wrongly think that once they have secured their patent, "the game's over." That the investment community will beat a path to their door, throwing money at them or some big company will come calling, begging to license or even acquire the technology. Does that happen? Sure, but so too does a blind squirrel, every now and then, find an acorn!

Entrepreneurs are often too focused on the concept or idea, not enough focused on developing the product or service to be created from the concept. Having patented intellectual property is a real advantage and is attractive to investors, but only if it has a practical implementation that has actual revenue or real potential. Intellectual property without any proof that it really works isn't even worth what it will cost you to file for it.

Make no mistake, a patent is important. It's simply no magic elixir. At the end of the day, having a working product with real customers and revenue is way more critical than simply patenting the intellectual property that underpins it. It proves that there is, in fact, real intellectual property! Whether that working product is built by others licensed by the patent holder or created and built by the entrepreneur who designed it, a practical plan (and notice I've used that ugly word, "practical" throughout – that's the critical part that many inventors miss). And then there's that nasty little issue of defending that patent and having the financial wherewithal to defend it.

So, three takeaways from this little discourse, assuming you have an invention worth patenting –

- Before you file for a patent, be sure that you have a plan for its ultimate implementation as a product;

- Know that once it is filed and approved, your design is in the public domain and is, potentially, vulnerable to "knockoffs" or copying;

- Know how you are going to defend it, should that be necessary (read capital and legal counsel). Either have a plan, whether it be with partners or distributors, to gain early and deep market share to drive revenue and deter new market entrants or know that there is capital available.

"If Failure is Not an Option...Then Neither is Success!"

How often have you heard the phrase "failure is not an option?" Nice strong words, good for effect, not good in reality, especially if want to be a successful entrepreneur.

Unfortunately, failure comes with the territory. And you have to be ready to face it...and be ready to rebound from it.

Sometimes, it's a big failure. Your whole business model doesn't work because you misjudged the ease of customer acceptance; or because of bad timing, be it with the economy as a whole, or a specific market, in particular. Sometimes, it's a smaller one, but nonetheless painful. You lose a big customer, simply because they chose a bigger supplier with a better price, discounting the value you brought them.

But many entrepreneurs look at failure as an ending, a devastation from which one can never recover. They continually try to ensure that they never make a mistake in their small business.

No one purposely seeks to fail. But it's not whether failure happens, but what you do with the opportunity that failure creates. It isn't an ending, but a beginning. A next step toward the ultimate success of your small business. And success almost can't happen without failure. And without failure, it's hard to really appreciate success. Plus, you can't play the game NOT TO LOSE!

It is said that Thomas Edison failed nearly 10,000 times before he got the light bulb right. Pete Rose had more than 4000 hits in his baseball career. He also made more than 8000 outs, more than most ballplayers had times at bat. Michael Jordan failed to hit the winning shot more than two dozen times, but we only remember the ones he made. Does anyone think of Mr. Edison, Mr. Rose or Mr. Jordan as failures?

In each case, with each failure, a lesson was learned and built upon. It's not that they failed, but what they did with each failure. Each failed attempt got Edison closer to his goal. Rose used each out as a learning experience for the next time he came to bat. Jordan's missed shots further fueled his competitive spirit for the next opportunity to win a game.

I have had many failures and they have all been learning experiences, albeit painful ones. Each one was almost like another course toward the degree in entrepreneurial success. For the entrepreneur, the road to success is paved with failures. Don't fear failure, but learn and grow from it.

"Want to Take on Long Odds? Try Introducing a New Product That's 'Better' Than an Established Product!"

Would-be entrepreneurs do it every day. They come up with a product concept that is "better" (and better is in quotes because often that is all relative) than an established product or brand already accepted and in use. And without deep pockets and lots of time, it becomes a Sisyphusian (big stone, steep hill) task.

This is often where entrepreneurs' passion (and ego) - their belief in their business concept and themselves is their undoing.

In their passion, they fail to realize what it will take to unseat a competitive product; how they will convince customers that their "better" is worth changing for. The established product is filling the customer need or solving the customer problem today. Maybe not perfectly, but sufficiently. With their ego, they believe they have created a product that is inherently "better" than their competitors' because they are smarter and have developed features that are cooler or sexier. That may be true, but customers rarely give style points!

All Startups Are Not Created Equal

Even for a "better" product to succeed, not only must its value (price/performance) be significantly better than what's out there, but the entrepreneur has to have a plan and the capital to back it up, to market and deliver it. Further, though, the competition isn't just going to sit back and watch. If any inroads are successful, they will mount a counter-attack (lower price, package differently, etc.), which only means more capital and more time required. And increasing odds for success.

So, what is an entrepreneur to do?

Don't do "better!" The capital requirements and time are too demanding and the chances for success too great for the entrepreneur. You want to introduce a new product? Find a pain point or customer need that's not being met today. Fill a niche not being served. Don't let your passion (belief in your concept) and your ego (I'm smarter than those guys) blind you. "Better" is a losing proposition. Find a way to do "new'...and "best!"

"Entrepreneurs Need to Learn How to Say 'No!'"

We all want to please. Entrepreneurs are no different. In fact, being so focused and passionate (to say nothing of having risk hanging over their head), they want nothing more than to please…their market, customers and employees alike to help their small business.

And so they make nearly-impossible-to-keep promises (which they do keep, usually at some huge personal or professional sacrifice), set nearly unattainable delivery schedules (which they usually make at the cost, often of their margin, and of nearly burning out themselves and those around them).

Unfortunately, it takes some hard experience (and usually a couple of expensive setbacks) to finally help the entrepreneur build a little harder edge. With that harder edge, finally comes the ability to say "no!" And that leads to the beginning of real growth …both for the entrepreneur and the small business.

"No, that prospect will take too many resources and too much time for too little revenue."

"No, we can't let you take that extra time off."

All Startups Are Not Created Equal

"No, we can't possibly meet that delivery requirement."

"No, our service offering doesn't include that."

"No, we won't reduce our price any further."

No, is the most critical word an entrepreneur can learn. Often, it means you won't get something you thought your company wanted or needed. But, it keeps you from "bet your company" decisions. It keeps you from veering off course to pursue business avenues that make no long-term sense. It keeps you humble, mindful that you (or company) can't do everything! It puts you in control of decisions…because they are not automatic!

"You Probably Have Not Discovered Fire! But If You Have, Your Work Has Just Begun!"

All too often I have encountered new entrepreneurs who tell me that their product is so unique that it has no competition and riches are just around the corner. As I explain to them, I believe fire has already been discovered (that's the last great invention that really had no precedent or competition)!

Now, there have certainly been "first movers" in every market space, but they are few and far between. And, typically, they are absolutely "right place, right time," kinds of businesses. First movers, who fit this classification in the last 10-15 years include Amazon, eBay, Yahoo, Google, Facebook, LinkedIn, Twitter just to name a few by example.

In the main, if you have a product or service that nobody's succeeded in bringing to market before, it, usually, doesn't mean that you're smarter or that nobody else has tried. I always tell entrepreneurs that somewhere out there are some much smarter guys in a garage who are doing what you're doing...only better and cheaper.

Most often it means that you haven't really done your homework. So, if you think you have such a product, your

All Startups Are Not Created Equal

work has just begun (and you thought developing the product was the hard part).

The first thing you need to do is research the market ...and then research some more, for past or present similar products/services and how the need you fulfill with your "breakthrough product" is being addressed today. And you can bet somebody did it before and probably failed. "Go to school on them" and find out why. Determine how your implementation of the idea is or can be significantly better than what was done in the past, or how you will fulfill the existing need better and cheaper.

Usually, you'll find that either the market need simply wasn't there; the market wasn't ready for the innovative product, or most probably that the guys who developed it ran out of money trying to educate the market on how much they needed the product/service. Most of the time, there is a need that is being fulfilled in a different way.

Years ago I had my first business in the early days of ATMs. People always needed access to their money and to transact basic banking business, but had been beaten down by bank policy to get used to the fact that they could only do it at their bank between 9 and 3 every weekday. The industry took more than fifteen years to develop, with the biggest obstacle the banks themselves, unwilling to change. Many of the original ATM manufacturers simply left the business or went out of business waiting for the market to unfold. And even today, with ATMs ubiquitous, and having always had the capability to perform virtually all basic transactions that were done at a teller window, they are still mostly cash machines.

So if you think you've "discovered fire," think again. Your work has just begun if your "fire" will ever see the light of day and have a chance at being successful. Research, stay open-minded (learn from your research) and think humbly (remember those real smart guys in the garage).

"Not All Startups Can Succeed, or... Even Passion and Hard Work Won't Overcome A Bad Business Concept!"

I can't tell you how many business plans I have read that were built on a business concept that simply could not work. Too often an entrepreneur, full of passion and bent on hard work, ventures out into a business that is either ill-conceived, poorly-timed or not well thought out.

Usually, it's an idea that just logically or theoretically makes sense to the entrepreneur, but has no shot in reality. It might have been that seminal "light bulb moment" when the idea came to entrepreneur. He/she then bounces the idea off of a couple of colleagues, who might also think the idea makes great sense ("great minds think alike" and all that). Then, armed simply with the idea, a sense of purpose and a strong work ethic, the entrepreneur sets off to conquer the world!

He/she might even meticulously create a business plan, complete with detailed financial projections of significant future revenue and profits. And, typically, the fundamental market analysis shows an equally significant market, built on the premise that because it's so logical, how could it not work? Even more typically, as the entrepreneur begins to introduce the concept to prospective customers and meets with courteous, if not tepid response, he/she just sees it as that minority of people who "don't get it." They continue down that wrong path, thinking that eventually hard work and their belief in their idea will win out.

But Master Yoda, didn't you tell us that passion and hard work are necessary for business success? Yes, that is true, but only if the business concept makes sense and can be proven.

Some telltale signs of a problematic business concept.

Often, the entrepreneur is a novice in the market(s) they are attempting to enter, feeling they are pioneers (or worse, "smarter" than the market) bringing a new idea to a market in need. Of course, they become more knowledgeable over time, but still remain naïve about the nuances of the market. Very typically, they don't seek out learned advice from "gray hairs" already in the business, mostly because they don't know enough about the market to even know who they are. As Disraeli cautions – "they don't know what they don't know!"

And finally, they have difficulty proving the concept in reality. In short, they find "the dogs just won't eat the dog food," or at least, not enough of them, even if they give "the dog food" away!

How does this happen?

Most often, the entrepreneur is so totally focused on the business idea and a sense of mission, that he/she never really took the time to answer the most basic questions that make an idea a business - **WHAT, WHERE, WHY** and **HOW!**

WHAT describes the fundamental problem to be addressed or the need to be fulfilled by the business' main product or service that is borne of the idea; how big that problem or need actually is.

All Startups Are Not Created Equal

WHERE describes the target market where the problem or need primarily exists.

WHY addresses why prospective customers will pay money for the **WHAT**.

HOW describes the steps (strategies, tactics and plans) that will be taken to get customers to buy the **WHAT**.

In the typical case of a bad business concept, the WHAT and WHY just never get addressed, but get painted with the logic and zeal of the entrepreneur, as opposed to solid research and market advice. A detailed business plan doesn't mean it was a well-thought out business concept or a business that can succeed. Just that the entrepreneur did some prolific writing. And more typically, they haven't engaged real market advice, understood real market situations and spoken with real potential customers to see if what they have can really become a scalable business.

Mostly their passion and sense of mission has convinced them they are right. Every entrepreneur needs to find knowledgeable folks who will be objective and point out the warts and blemishes that envelop their business concept and their product/service. Every business/product/service has them. To the extent they can't be overcome will be the determining factor for whether the business actually has "legs" to proceed.

And sometimes it just doesn't. I preach passion, but all the passion in the world cannot overcome a poorly thought-out business concept or one where the market just isn't right, whether it be economic conditions (like the last several years) or market conditions (too early or not a big enough problem). Then it may be time to move on to something else.

There are countless stories of learning from early failure breeding later success - quitting, then trying again, later. Either with a concept that is better thought out by answering the WHAT, WHERE, WHY and HOW questions, or one where the timing is better.

"It's Lonely at the Top... Guidance for the Early Stage CEO"

So you proved your concept. You have some actual customers, driving real revenue and maybe even have an employee or two. Have enough funding to last a little while, but some nagging doubts. You've never done this before. In fact, you've never really run a business. And now here you are, all alone, trying to figure out how to take that concept, those few customers, that couple of employees and create a sustaining, scalable business.

Yikes! Now is when you really become an entrepreneur!

When customers and employees are depending on the decisions you make. It's a scary time. B-school didn't prepare for this. All those case studies never mentioned midnight calls from your website developer whose system crashed and won't be able to roll out the new website that your already-implemented email campaign is counting on. Or when one of your key employees (at this point they're all key) decides that she really doesn't like "life on the fault line," and is taking a more secure job back in a big company. Trust me, we've all faced it. But you don't have to face it alone... or without guidance. So let Yoda help.

- **Get an advisor or mentor.** Somebody you can bounce ideas off of, or to whom you can bring problems to help you solve. In fact, if you can, set up an advisory board of three or four folks, who you respect, who've been to the same dance you're at right now. Entrepreneurs, small business owners, call them what you will. Folks who've had to make payrolls. Who've faced the midnight calls. The employee desertions. The collection problems. The IRS. But if you can only find one, make sure it's one who you trust, because if you trust he/she, you will listen to them. And that is the most critical part of having advisors. (More on this in the next chapter).

- **Be totally market and customer-focused.** If you have existing customers, smother them with service. Create their undying loyalty. They will be your best salespeople. Know your competition as well as you know your own company and product (and if you tell me you have none, I'll tell you, you ain't paying attention). You will learn what's made them successful and what you need to do to beat them in the marketplace. Go to industry trade shows (notice I didn't say exhibit – waste of time and money for the small company). Carry "your booth" in your backpack. Meet prospects, listen to the "rhythm" of the marketplace. Review competitors, especially the newer ones. You'll learn the most from other hungry folks like you.

- **Find partners.** Many entrepreneurs believe that raising capital is the key to early business success. I say partially true. You raise capital to acquire resources (people, technology, real estate, etc.) that helps you grow. Well, why not just partner with folks who have those resources already rolling and take out the middleman (capital). Partners can help you build your product through a technology licensing deal; sell your product through a sales distribution relationship or even support your product through a help desk relationship. In the early going, it helps avoid the staffing, training, growing phase and moves right into the actual executing.

- **Create a business plan.** Not some masterpiece worthy of a Pulitzer, but a "battle plan" for attacking your market, beating your competition and winning new customers and growing your business. It can be a ten page set of objectives and strategies; a three page outline of key tasks or a big white board assembly of customer, product and support initiatives. Key thing is that it totally describe how you operate on a day-to-day basis. What's important to do and track. Nothing more, nothing less.

- **Have an outlet.** Whether it's family, running or just sitting on the beach. Have a place, hopefully with people you love, where you can decompress and re-charge. You can't run even the best sports car non-stop for long periods without servicing or you'll have serious problems. Same thing with your life. Your business should only be a part of your life, albeit a major one, but you'll be a better owner and a better person if you are able to let it go of it, periodically.

Welcome to our fraternity, new entrepreneur. Sure, it's lonely at the top... but it doesn't have to be. Reach out. Help is on the way!

Chapter 2 – Don't Just Have a Clue. Have a Strategy…and a Plan!

"If Your Business Doesn't Have a Plan, You May Soon Not Have a Business!"

Much has been written about the need for a business plan. But most often it's in the context of a document that's used to raise money, often creating a masterpiece of dazzling charts and colors, with writing often worthy of a Pulitzer Prize. But the long and the short of it is that developing a business plan may be the second most important task in creating a foundation for success for an entrepreneur. An army wouldn't go into battle without a battle plan. Nor should a business. And while, it, ultimately, may help you get necessary funding, it should provide a roadmap for how the business will operate from day one and be continually updated as business and market conditions dictate. It should be a living, breathing document.

And what is the MOST important task in creating a foundation for success for an entrepreneur? It's the execution of that plan! There, are, literally, thousands upon thousands of great business plans, but only hundreds upon hundreds of great executions!

So let's start. Forget the pretty templates. Just get to the basics and keep it simple.

Don't Just Have a Clue. Have a Strategy...and a Plan!

First, be able to simply describe your business concept. For this, use my "Aunt Tilly Rule." Be able to describe your business in one or two sentences so that even your elderly Aunt Tilly can comprehend your business concept. This should encompass what it is you do (products and/or services), to what target market, to solve what market need. Once you've done this (and you will be constantly modifying it as your business evolves) you now have a crisp definition that you can use when you meet prospective customers, suppliers or, ultimately, investors. Plus, if Aunt Tilly can understand it...so will they!

Next, know your battlefield – its topography, enemies and allies: Understand your target market(s), your ideal customer profile, your competition and potential strategic partners. Define, research and size your market as thoroughly as you can. And remember your market should be defined by the your ideal customer – that is, the customer whose needs your product or service meet as well or better than anything out there today.

Define and describe your product(s) and/or service(s). What features, functions, most importantly what benefits it/they offer your target market – how it/they fulfill the needs described, previously.

Establish three year financial goals, monthly for the first year, quarterly for the second and third. These will be the yardsticks you measure against. And a caution here. With tongue, firmly planted in cheek, please make sure these goals are on paper, as opposed to etched in stone. Easier to change them that way...and they surely will need to be changed as market and business conditions dictate. But they remain the scoreboard of your business plan execution.

Further, develop a simple set of strategies and tactics that have as their foundation how to most effectively deliver your product(s) and/or service(s) to your target market to meet your financial goals. They have to be connected.

Essential in these strategies and tactics are marketing and sales. In short, how will you create awareness and interest in your product(s) and/or service(s) and how you will convert those qualified leads into actual sales. You can develop other strategies and tactics regarding operations, customer support and organizational development, but if you focus on sales and marketing, you're focused on the most important elements of the business – customers and revenue. The rest just supports those two.

Establish short-term milestones regarding key tasks in product development and strategy and tactical implementation and manage them tightly.

Finally, once more, keep it simple but direct. Document it, live with it and, above all else, focus on its implementation. It is your bible, your battle plan, your livelihood. In a later chapter, we'll talk about how to turn this battle plan into a plan to raise funding.

Don't Just Have a Clue. Have a Strategy...and a Plan!

"Without Objectives, There Can Be No Real Strategies and without Real Strategies There Can Be No Long-Term Success!"

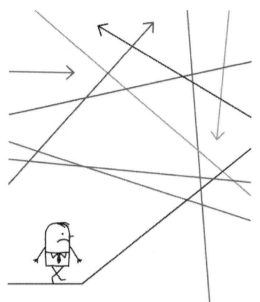

I'm rarely contacted by a prospective client unless they are in trouble, real or perceived. Most often, their lament is that their growth has slowed or even stopped. And my first question usually is "what's the basis for your growth - that is, why do you want/need to grow?"

Now if that sounds like a strange question, think about it. Growth for growth's sake is meaningless. You should grow for a reason or reasons – gain economies of scale to generate more profitability; or gain the capital to expand your product set, or increase your customer base to create a basis for selling a broader product set into that base, to name a few. Or something as simple as attracting a more experienced management team or even, as a business owner you can take more cash out of the business. There are no meaningless objectives. They are the targets the business aims to meet over time. And it is upon these objectives that the strategies for the business are based. They are what gives the business direction.

A few months back in one of my postings, I attempted to show startup businesses the value of having a business plan. Yet, once beyond the startup phase, few businesses or business owners have a set of objectives upon which they operate and upon which they build strategies, let alone an ongoing business plan. In fact, few, if any small business owners who've been in business for longer than a couple of years, do much planning or objective setting beyond, maybe, putting together an annual budget or forecast. And without specific objectives and strategies, the business, in good times, will wander. And in bad, will flounder.

So when the challenges of an economy like the one we've been in for the last several years occur, the business, in the absence of any firm targets or strategies to get there, begins operating in a "strategy du jour" mode, continually trying to come up with something that works for them, but has no real basis, except trying something new. In the process they waste precious resources and slow "growth" (the only vague objective they might have) even more. As with the old saying, "if you don't know where you're going, most any road will take you there."

As the business owner, what do you do?

Well, do what I do when I first walk into a new client situation and before we go very far into the engagement. I ask them to take a step back and ask themselves the following questions:

- Where do I, specifically, want the business to be over the next 3 years, and why?

- Where do I, specifically, want to be personally, professionally and financially over the next 3 years and why?

Don't Just Have a Clue. Have a Strategy...and a Plan!

I tell them to ask the first question of their key people, as well, especially those in a management role. Get a consensus. On the second question, which, of course, is closely tied to the first, I tell them to ask their significant other or even close friends to help them. Get a consensus here as well.

Just by addressing these simple questions and coming up with some basic, straightforward objectives, the business (and the business owner) now has a foundation and rationale for the strategies it creates and decisions it makes to implement those strategies. It could help better rationalize when, where and how to grow the business as well as potentially exit it. As external factors, like the economy or markets change, adjustments can be made, accordingly, that still keep the business heading in the right direction...for the right reasons.

If this all sounds so mundane and fundamental, it is. But, as Yoda has said many times in these postings, success in most any endeavor - business, sports or life, for that matter, is based on getting the fundamentals right. And they're never very exciting, but they ALWAYS work!

"Ready, Fire, Aim! How Premature Execution Dooms a Good Plan."

Just as the Christmas shopping season was coming to a close, there was an announcement from BestBuy, the huge "big box" retailer, that it had cancelled an undisclosed number of orders because it did not have the inventory to fulfill them. On the surface, beyond the fact that it was during the high volume holiday shopping period, not earth-shattering news. But, go just below the surface to understand why, and it's a really big deal.

Why did it occur?

They offered deep discounts on certain items as a competitive thrust against Amazon.com and Wal-Mart stores. Best Buy promoted "'aggressively online,' leading to higher traffic and an increase in sales by stores open at least 14 months," their CEO noted.

Now let's think about this. First, they discounted, lowering margins on certain products. Second, they succeeded in driving more traffic and, you would then think, more revenue (less profitable, but more of it). Third, however, they appear to have not planned to be successful, since they didn't properly forecast inventory requirements for that success. Fourth, this caused a double jeopardy situation. Reduced margins, and because they couldn't fulfill orders, reduced revenue.

Don't Just Have a Clue. Have a Strategy...and a Plan!

How does a company let that happen?

This is a classic case of the "ready, fire, aim" syndrome that exists in far too many businesses today, and one that can cost small business owners more than just the "bad press" that BestBuy had to endure.

"Ready, fire, aim" is really a case of a good plan gone bad, not through bad execution, just premature execution. Usually, for a small business, this occurs for one of two reasons. Overreaction – where a plan is thrown together and hastily implemented because the entrepreneur panics. Or worse, a good plan is put together and then either prematurely or poorly executed. In either case, the small business owner, in their desire to "make something happen" becomes impatient and moves forward before they should.

In the case of BestBuy, my guess is that they did some "eleventh hour tweaking" of their discounting (probably reducing it even further) and never took into account the inventory implications of this last minute tweak and what it would do to customers' jumping at the offers.

How often have you done the same thing in your own business? Either not waiting to completely develop market roll-out plans, moving up or condensing schedules, or doing last minute, poorly thought-out "tweaks," because "we need the revenue?"

Patience is not, typically, an entrepreneurial virtue. But sometimes, doing it "by the numbers," not only makes good sense, but, most often, if the plan is sound, leads to success. The downside is usually disastrous.

So, how do you avoid the "Ready, Fire, Aim" syndrome? Here are some key bits of advice when making a major marketing thrust, be it a new product introduction, new packaging or a new pricing scheme:

- **Develop a simple, but comprehensive, market roll-out plan**

Clearly defined steps, milestones and critical roles and responsibilities of all of those involved.

- **Determine the operational implications of market success**

At various levels of success (from just okay to wildly), what will be the impact on operations, customer support, etc.? Will you be able to fulfill the promise of the marketing campaign?

- **Execute with the precision of a military campaign**

Don't allow good planning to be done in by poor execution. Planning is less than half the battle. Execution IS the battle! Make sure there is someone responsible for managing the myriad tasks of plan implementation (and that it's not you, the owner).

Too many good strategic or marketing ideas become hastily drawn-up plans. Too many good strategic or marketing plans become poorly or prematurely executed. Be watchful and remember it's "Ready, Aim, Fire!"

Don't Just Have a Clue. Have a Strategy...and a Plan!

"Never Waste a Time at Bat! Good Advice in Baseball, Even Better in Small Business!"

My avocation is baseball, where I coached at every conceivable level for nearly thirty years. My prime focus was teaching hitting. Now, hitting a baseball, especially at a high level of competition, is, perhaps, one of the single most difficult things to do. When a hitter is ready to hit ("at bat," for those of you not familiar with the game), he is facing a pitcher who may have a half a dozen different pitches that he can throw, at least one or two in the 90+ mph range, trying to get his pitch past the hitter, either with speed, guile or location. Add a screaming crowd and the hitter has some real challenges. And my advice to the hitter? Have a plan for every single at bat. Never waste one. Determine how to approach that specific pitcher in that specific situation. You can never tell when that one at bat, might be the game changer.

The same thing holds true for entrepreneurs and small business owners.

In opportunities for sales, partnering or investment, you have to have a plan, well thought-out and then well executed. Because, you often face formidable competition, much larger partners and investors who have preconceived notions. And, you can never tell when that opportunity might be the game changer for your small business. Further, you never know when it might be your only (or last) chance to be in front of that individual or company. And that's how you should treat every single instance for a sale, a partner or investment.

Entrepreneurs don't often consider that approach. It's most especially important because the population of the various targeted areas (for sale, partner or investment) is not limitless. In fact, for partner or investment there could be but just a few opportunities available that fit a particular business.

So here's some guidance and questions to ask yourself about how to approach an opportunity so that you "never waste a time at bat":

- **Know Your Audience**
It's like knowing the pitcher; what pitch he throws in what situation. How much do you know about the individual or company that represents the opportunity? What's their individual or company background? What have they done, how have they have reacted, in the past, in a similar situation? What are their "hot buttons" – those things that they feel strongest about?

- **Create a Plan**
What are you going to present, how and why? How will it meet the needs, requirements or profile of the targeted audience? What's going to make them want to do business with you?

- **Be Prepared**

Don't Just Have a Clue. Have a Strategy…and a Plan!

Executing a plan is not just completing a series of tasks. It's meeting the objectives of the plan, sometimes, in ways not envisioned by the key tasks. Sometimes, you have to react to new data, new people, new requirements, "on the fly." To do this, you have to be ready, not just with a rehearsed presentation, but with potential "what if's" that might come up during your meeting(s). Being prepared engenders confidence. Confidence breeds success.

Approach every key sales, partnering or investment opportunity like it might be your last chance. It also might end up be a game changer for you. Never waste a time at bat!

"Are You Building a Business That's '80 Miles Wide and An Inch Deep?'"

It never ceases to amaze me how many small business owners think that having multiple sources of revenue, often across multiple market types is a good business model. Or having products that seemingly have application across a series of vertical markets and attempting to penetrate all of them. They argue that with many different ways to make money, they increase their odds for success. Because it makes logical sense to extend their product reach or to expand their market, that they should do it. Nope! In fact, it's a really good vehicle to get yourself to a business exit...and not in a good way!

These are folks I accuse of having a business that's "80 miles wide and an inch deep." Lots of breadth, no depth. For entrepreneurs, resources are typically not in abundance. So instead of maniacally focusing those resources on one or two key applications where either their product fits well (addresses key pain points of potential customers) or find a niche in which they can be a leader, preferably both, they diffuse those resources across many. Whether that be technology resources creating feature after feature or sales and marketing resources, selling into markets or customer sets that are widely diverse.

Small business success, especially in the early years, is dependent on focus. Yet I have seen countless companies

Don't Just Have a Clue. Have a Strategy...and a Plan!

drive themselves from profitability to the brink of bankruptcy, by either over-expanding or thinking they can be "all things to all people." Focus means finding a niche you can own and then penetrating it, trying to capture as much of it as possible, best leveraging limited resources.

Are you guilty of lack of focus? Here are some considerations that may prove your guilt!

Because you can, doesn't mean you should.
You've added or are adding product features because they're easy, because you think they are logical extensions of your product line, or worse, because they are "sexy" features that show your technological prowess, all without really determining the market potential or impact.

More is not better it is only more!
You have added multiple variations of product packages or pricing over the last year or two in hopes of creating more appeal across a wider set of customers, not understanding that you have to have a value proposition for those customers, regardless of packaging or pricing.

...And it can also make your coffee in the morning!
Your product has so many features and functions (which you drive home, relentlessly in every piece of literature) that it even sales and marketing people's "eyes glaze over" as they try to first understand all of them, and second, try to understand how to turn them into customer benefits

Bring me your tired, your poor, your huddled masses...!
You believe your product is so complete that it serves the needs of a broad set of vertical market segments, and you set out to go after all of them, not understanding that you have to have sales presence in all those market segments to even begin to penetrate them.

Focus, focus, focus. That is the essence of success. And the essence of focus is a deep understanding and penetration of niche markets where you can succeed. And, developing and delivering products and their associated features and functions that best meet the needs of the customers in those niche markets.

Doing one thing exceptionally well, is far better than doing many things, adequately!

Don't Just Have a Clue. Have a Strategy...and a Plan!

"Being Small May Well be Your Biggest Asset!"

Many entrepreneurs are most defensive about the fact that their company is small, or worse, intimidated by the fact that their competitors are large. When, if truth be told, their size can be their biggest asset.

History is littered with stories of how small, yet nimble bands of guerilla fighters with a deep belief in their mission, have often, out-maneuvered, out-thought and defeated larger, better equipped armies. In the United States' formative years, a rag-tag group of dedicated militiamen defeated a British Army that often outnumbered them by 10 to 1.

If you were to find commonality in history where small defeated large you would find four main characteristics – an unbending belief in the mission, selective engagement (the essence of guerilla fighting and the subject of a previous blog post), flexibility to "think outside the box" and agility to be able to mobilize and strike quickly. And by applying these same principles, the small business can succeed, time and again in competitive encounters!

Let's consider each and how you can apply them in your situation.

Unbending Belief in Your Mission

This is simply passion, of which I've spoken many times. And it, obviously, goes without saying, but you'd be surprised by how many small business owners "stop believing" in times of competitive adversity. "Rolling over" or declining to work a situation because of an entrenched competitor, even though they have a better product and better pricing. As the oft-used Journey song goes, "Don't Stop Believing!"

Selective Engagement

Again, another subject about which I've spoken before. But, in a nutshell, it means to pick and choose those situations where the odds are best for victory. You don't, necessarily walk away from a battle because you can't win, but because you can't fight all the battles. Being, small, you are resource-constrained, so use your resources wisely.

Flexibility

This is the ability to find a way to "change the rules" of engagement. Now, of course, you can't change the "market rules," but you sure can adjust the playing field but doing something completely "out of the box" that favors you.

For example, I have a company that I advise, who is one of the smallest players in a market dominated by one major player. This large company has dictated a pricing policy that is not only "a la carte," for products and services, but tends to low-ball initial bids and then counts on "add-ons" after the contract is signed to get the price up into the stratosphere. Other competitors have followed suit. The only losers were the customers.

So my client decided to change the rules.

They established a "single line" price that "changed the rules," made them stand out and made things more difficult for competitive comparison. Results? A series of competitive wins because the competition wouldn't or couldn't (see below) react.

Agility

This is simply being able to react quickly to either market opportunities or changing market conditions. Typically, a large company has a specific way of doing business, often documented by a book of processes and procedures (not that this is wrong) that makes changing strategies or tactics akin to turning a battleship or getting a law passed through Congress. But the small company operates by more simple dictums (like survival) that help it to better react to specific situations.

I had another small company client that was able to announce, roll-out and secure customers with a new product offering that capitalized on recently-passed legislation that enabled them to capture market share a solid six months before any competitive response. By being quick and nimble they created a market lead, and while their competitive edge eroded over time, they never lost.

Use your passion. Pick your battles. Be flexible...but smart. Be nimble where competition is plodding. These are the keys to small beating large. These are the keys to making your size your biggest asset.

"Adapt or Die! React to Market Changes before They Force Change on You."

During a recent Christmas season, I was listening to a news report about how "Cyber Monday" was expected to just "blow the doors" off of prior years' and this year's forecasted holiday shopping dollar volume (and, of course, it did). Juxtaposed with that report was that of a couple small business owners who were interviewed and were whining about how the internet was just killing their business and they would probably be closing after the holiday season.

Now let's see. Do you think they just woke up that morning and came to that realization? No, I don't think so. The internet as retail presence has been around for more than ten years and "Cyber Monday" as a retail force for more than five. So did these small retailers just figure they would go away as a competitive threat, even after seeing volume dramatically increasing, year after year? The signs were there. They simply chose to ignore them. And now, it might be too late. They may have become dinosaurs!

Unfortunately, too few entrepreneurs pay enough attention to what is going on in and around their market, what may be coming, and what outside influences (like the internet was in the late 90s) might impact their business, dramatically, in the future. The landscape is littered with successful companies who, like the dinosaur, did not pay attention and then, could not adapt.

How about Blockbuster? It took them too long to recognize that the future was in downloading movies and that their bricks and mortar and DVD rental models were going to be outdated. They're still around, but a mere shadow of their former selves. Another would be Research in Motion (RIM) and their Blackberry. They owned the PDA/Smart Phone market (at one point more than 75%) but with a very narrow viewpoint of where that market was going. Then along came Apple's iPhone and Google's Android operating system and, over a couple of years, the mobile phone was a personal communication device with millions of applications available for it. And the Blackberry is struggling for not just market share (now less than 20%) but for relevance.

This is a frequent story for many small businesses, where market forces change or big competitors enter, or both. But, typically, it doesn't happen overnight. There's usually plenty of advanced warning of the changes or new entries. Time enough to watch and study how these changes might impact an entrepreneur's business model. Then determine that if things appear to be drastically changing for the future, a new strategy is going to be necessary to compete and maybe, to survive. That might entail, even "re-inventing the company."

The best example, today for a company that re-invented itself has to be Apple. By the late 70s, it had engineered one of the first commercially available lines of personal computers. By the early-to-mid 80s, it owned that market.

Then, it ignored and/or underestimated the changes going on all around it (PC clones, the spread of Windows applications, etc.) and proceeded to become an "also ran" used by educators and a cult of loyal users. Then (with the return of Steve Jobs) it re-invented itself as a consumer digital products company, transforming music, mobile phones and personal computing, along the way.

Now, as a small business owner, facing major market changes or competitor inroads, you aren't (and probably don't have a) Steve Jobs. Nor do you have the resources of an Apple. However, that doesn't mean you can't "think different." Not just outside the box, but inside it as well (we're often so busy thinking outside the box, we miss what is right in front of us).

Look to where are you most vulnerable, be that in a specific market segment, product feature/function or product delivery/support. Determine, initially, how can you fortify that area (develop plans to protect). At the same time, think of ways you can "change the rules" – find new methods to package or price your product that are way different than the market is used to. Maybe deliver it in ways or with services, no one has done before.

As an example, how about those whining retailers? What could they have done over the last 5-10 years to have altered their vulnerability? Maybe they could have established their own internet presence. Maybe they could have changed the focus of their business, becoming much more specialized with a tighter niche they could own, or offering a service or support level not seen in their market segment, previously. They could have done many things to survive...except nothing.

Don't Just Have a Clue. Have a Strategy…and a Plan!

Know that you will, at some point, face market disruption. Whatever you do, stay vigilant. Be aware of market changes and competitive inroads and react to them BEFORE they become major threats to your customer base and your revenue.

"And What Happens to the Business If You Get Hit by a Bus?"

What would happen to your small business if you were suddenly removed from it...for whatever reason? How much thought have you ever given to the potential of that happening? What if one day, you, the chief entrepreneur, business architect and visionary, became incapacitated...or just ceased to be?

Sorry to be a purveyor of gloom and doom, but this is often the last thing any entrepreneur thinks about. But the implications of losing its leader, not just for the small business, its shareholders, employees and its future, but the personal, family and professional ramifications could be earth-shattering.

Now, I'm not talking about having key-man insurance (but even in that case, let's see those Benjamin Franklins step in and take over for you on day 1 after you're not there), or some kind of succession plan, but having a true fallback plan in case of something happens to you, where you can no longer drive the company. Everything you worked for up to that point could be in jeopardy! It's even more disastrous than dying without a will. At least Probate Court will sort that out for you. Nobody sorts out what happens to a leaderless small business.

Don't Just Have a Clue. Have a Strategy…and a Plan!

And the longer you've been in business, the more difficult it becomes not just for the business itself, but its shareholders/partners, employees, customers and suppliers. Since 9/11 many businesses have put together some form of disaster recovery plan to ensure that in time of a major external event that impacts the business, it has a plan to continue. Think of your fallback plan as a disaster recovery plan for the worst kind of disaster a small business can encounter…the loss of its entrepreneurial leader. Unthinkable? If 9/11 taught us anything, it taught us that the unthinkable can happen!

Answer some key questions. Who will take over? Why? How? When? Does anybody know all that you know? If not, why not? Discuss the potential situation with key shareholders or board members, if you have them; your accountant; your lawyer; key employees, family members. Document it, however rudimentary, and give it to several folks you trust, for safekeeping and work with your attorney on the steps necessary to execute it, should that be necessary.

Don't waste another minute. Put it together, now, today. Your shareholders/partners, employees and your family will thank you.

Chapter 3 – There's Safety in Numbers! Look for Partners and Advisors

"Partner Your Way to Success"

Often, entrepreneurs are so intently focused on finding ways to build their business or raising capital that they overlook key avenues to address both needs. Partnering is one of most important vehicles available to an entrepreneur, especially in the early stages of the business, where you can leverage scarce resources to either generate revenue or conserve expenses, or both. It can potentially provide valued visibility in the marketplace both with the strategic partners as well as with potential future customers. Yet few entrepreneurs capitalize on the many opportunities that exist for them to partner.

Strategic partnerships can fulfill a number of functions for the small business owner. They can provide expanded sales coverage with the partner selling the entrepreneur company's product or service into markets where there is significant potential and applicability but where the entrepreneur has no presence (and the partner does).

Or, a partner can provide needed development resources to enable the entrepreneur company to complete a new product, in return for exclusive use of that product in the partner's target (and non-competitive) market space. Here the entrepreneur wins twice. Gets development resources they didn't have and exposure (and potential new revenue) in markets they never expected.

There's Safety in Numbers! Look for Partners and Advisors

Finally, a partner can provide add-on product for entrepreneur to expand its offerings into its existing market, providing additional opportunities for revenue without expending additional resources for development.

But where do you find partners?

They come in all shapes and sizes. They could be larger companies that are operating in the same (but non-competitive) market space that the entrepreneurial company is. Or they could be another small company that has strengths where you have weaknesses. For example, they are strong in development or engineering and you are stronger in manufacturing or sales. In essence, seek a complement, to your needs and requirements, whether that be market penetration, or expansion or to your product mix.

Early on in your company's life, look for ways to expand sales distribution or product development. Seek opportunities to get more for less, thereby, reducing capital requirements and preserving cash. Later in the company's development, look to partnering for chances to get enter new markets or expand your product line, providing market expansion without expansion capital. And finally, a good strategic partner can, eventually, become an even better strategic buyer, potentially providing you an optimum exit opportunity.

What are you waiting for? Go find a partner. Your success could depend on it!

"Free Advice Is Usually Worth What You Pay For It!"

Some time ago, a question was raised in one of the discussion groups on LinkedIn about the value of mentoring as one of the most critical elements in contributing to the success of small business owners. It helps entrepreneurs to avoid the pitfalls and mistakes that the advisor/mentor has made in their own careers.

It further provides objectivity in assisting the small business owner with key decision-making and should help provide a "sounding board" and even a basis for new ideas for the business' success. Moreover, it provides a factor of accountability that the entrepreneur only gets, otherwise, from the mirror.

Having started and sold multiple businesses and been a CEO for more than 30 years across different industries, I have advised or mentored many entrepreneurs and future business owners. However, by and large, I realized what I was doing wasn't working either for me or the entrepreneur. I have painfully learned and firmly believe that, most often, "free advice is worth what you pay for it." I used to give free advice, freely. Consequently, I was continually frustrated by providing guidance and observations that, ultimately, were ignored and watched the entrepreneur make the mistake(s) that I warned were going to be the outcome of their direction

There's Safety in Numbers! Look for Partners and Advisors

or decision. Further, it wasted both of our times, without any good result.

Now, by and large, I mostly provide the same good advice for a fee, to a decidedly smaller group of businesses. But they listen, because they are paying for it, not outrageously, but enough that they think twice before engaging my efforts and then not paying attention to the advice. That's what makes this kind of advising work for both sides. "Win, win."

Selectively, I still mentor raw startups, pro bono, who have limited capital but a deep passion for a business model that I believe can succeed. For them, I have set three rules. First, my time, like theirs is valuable, use it with discretion. Second, some day they may be able to afford me, but for now not to worry about paying. But at some point in the future, do this for someone else...in essence, "pay it forward." And finally, listen. They don't have to accept my advice, blindly, but, at least, consider it. Again, a "win, win."

In either case, there is a price and there is a return. Value for value.

However, regardless of whether it's for fee or for free, the essence of successful mentoring relationship is that it have some agreed upon objectives over some finite time horizon. And that it be judged, on both sides, by the results against those objectives. This forces accountability on the small business owner and dedication on the part of the mentor/advisor.

"'Tap the Gray Hair!' – Creating and Using an Advisory Board/Board of Directors"

Every entrepreneur needs mentoring and advisors. You can't get enough good advice. A board can be forum for that advice. And there are more than enough grizzled veterans with gray hair to tap to feel out that board. However, at the end of day, how deep and what you get out of a board really depends on how you want to use your advisors.

There are two types of boards that you can use - an advisory board or a board of directors.

Typically, an advisory board is an ad hoc group that you might meet with or talk to either, individually, or as a group, primarily as a sounding board. You can always use an advisory board. These folks will make themselves available, as necessary, but it usually won't be on a formal schedule or setting. Plus, a typical advisory board, at least early on, will provide that advice for free.

Two-edged sword. There will, usually, be a limit to how much time these advisors will give you, since they are doing it gratis (although, you might find folks who enjoy the mentoring so much, that they give advice whenever and

There's Safety in Numbers! Look for Partners and Advisors

wherever requested). Second, a word of warning. Always remember, unfortunately, "free advice is worth what you pay for it." With no real basis and no stake in the venture, much of the advice can be both "out-of context," "off the cuff" and often not relevant. You need only go to some of entrepreneur group social networking sites and ask advice to prove this one.

As your business rolls out and grows, you will need a board of directors, at a minimum, as a post-fact review group and broad-based sounding board. Often this group is made up the company's accountant and/or lawyer and maybe a trusted friend or advisor. While these folks will have a fiduciary responsibility to the shareholders, early on that's probably just you and maybe a few of your colleagues or family members (who may have put some money up). Later, that will get more complicated, but let's just concentrate on starting.

Often though, companies make the mistake of trying to have both, when they can actually combine the best of both, reducing complexity and noise.

If your plan is that your advisors are going to be an active sounding board and part of helping you set and implement the strategic direction of the company, then you might think about forming a small board of directors with no more than three or four individuals, to keep it manageable. (You can add your accountant or lawyer, but, frankly, unless they really understand your business, they won't add much and you can always invite them to board meetings.) You should further consider three things in your selection – geography, experience and compensation. Let's address each one.

Geography

Geography in your proposed directors' role is very important, because you (and they) would want frequent face time to help understand and monitor the strategies and plans in which they would be involved, especially in the early going. So you want them within a reasonable geographic radius from where your company is. Plus, you avoid either the director having to "eat" travel expenses or the company incurring those expenses (see my comment on cash flow below).

Experience
Experience is a given, but don't make the mistake of either a "big name" or a "big company" guy (or gal). I have learned, in creating and serving on boards for more than 30 years, that for startups you need former entrepreneurs, who "have been there." Specifically, you should look for advisors with expertise in taking products to market, establishing strategic relationships, raising money or developing/executing various business strategies for small companies. All of these are critical skills, plus most former small businessmen have strong feelings about the importance of managing cash. That is one of the most critical skills.

Compensation
Finally, relative to compensation, as per my previous comment about free advice, there needs to be compensation, but, if possible, keep cash payments to a minimum. It can be all over the lot, but that said entrepreneurs, with their respect for cash flow, will, more often than not, accept mostly, if not all, "paper" compensation - i.e., options, warrants, etc. (so long as they are delivered in such a way as to not create a taxable event for the director – your accountant can help with that). Two good things about this form of compensation. First, it means that what the board member is bringing to the table is being respected. Second, it means that board member also has a "stake" in the success of

There's Safety in Numbers! Look for Partners and Advisors

enterprise. Between these two elements, it also means that you can, virtually, tap this advice, whenever and wherever necessary, and that will be invaluable.

Go find that gray hair...and use it to your best advantage!

"Is Your Nose Pressed Right Up Against a Tree as You Are Trying to See the Forest?"

Every small business owner knows that above all else, you need to be maniacally-focused to succeed. Because of this, for the entrepreneur, oftentimes, keeping things in perspective is extraordinarily difficult. You live and breathe the business, day in and day out, dealing with customers, employees and suppliers. However, you often can't objectively understand product or marketing shortcomings. Opportunities may pop out of unusual circumstances, but if they don't pop right in front of you, you may miss them. When problems occur, often they come as a surprise, and their solutions elusive. Most of the time, the problem should have been apparent, but wasn't and its solution, while readily available, was ignored.

Unfortunately, most small business owners suffer "a forest for the trees" problem. They are so focused on what is right in front of them, that anything on the periphery is lost. They are looking into a distorted mirror for answers.

Does this describe you and your business?

If so, how do you keep a balance so that you can maintain objectivity and recognize opportunities or problems as they occur, without losing focus on moving the business forward?

There's Safety in Numbers! Look for Partners and Advisors

You need to seek a trusted advisor or group of advisors to provide you, at a minimum, an objective mirror on your business and, ultimately, to hold you accountable for what is going on, in and around your enterprise.

Maybe it's something as simple as a periodic breakfast with a friend, who may be a former colleague or a more experienced former entrepreneur, just to "vent," describing what's been happening in your business since you last met that is frustrating you. For the simple price of a breakfast, you may gain an insight or an idea that you wouldn't have otherwise gotten that might help you look at things a little differently or help make a change you might not have thought of.

Or, it could be something more formal like an advisory board made up of individuals who bring to your business both small business experience and/or functional expertise that you lack. This will cost you more than a breakfast, but it will be well worth it (see my previous post regarding "free advice being worth what you pay for it"). How you structure it and how frequently you meet are really up to you. However, whether it be an individual or a board, there are five key factors to consider relative to establishing a trusted advisor relationship:

Small Business Experience
Sorry, just because Uncle Ned will listen to your problems, the fact that he was an audit manager for Fortune 500 company for 40 years, says he won't be able to relate and therefore, not bring much to the party. While it is helpful, they don't have to have experience in your market sector or business type, but do seek out folks who have "had to make a payroll."

Functional Expertise (especially in areas where you are weak)

If your background is strong in sales and marketing, but you have no feel for "the numbers," an advisor with a strong finance background can really provide insights that you might never have discovered on your own.

Benchmark Position or Plan (and the willingness to share it)

You need to have a relative starting point to give your trusted advisor(s) a perspective as to where you are and what you are trying to accomplish. This should be documented and should contain as much detail as you feel comfortable sharing (but you need to be both honest and willing to share – they are either "trusted" or they're not). While you can verbally present it over pancakes and sausages, if they have something they can refer to either at the initial meeting and later, they can ask questions that might not have been evident in just your verbal outline. Plus, it gives them a way to track progress and ask about how you are doing relative to certain objectives or strategies that you initially presented.

Your Willingness to Listen to Criticism and New Perspectives (and the desire to change)

If you think you have all the answers, don't waste your time with advisors. You need to be willing to have some individual or group hold you accountable. To be able to listen to the potential that you might be doing something wrong from someone who has way more experience, expertise or objectivity than you do. Further, they might bring value by presenting a contrarian view to a potential strategy you are considering that might work even better than the one you have developed.

Compensation (agreed upon at the outset)

There's Safety in Numbers! Look for Partners and Advisors

This is always a knotty issue for entrepreneurs, especially when it involves potential cash. Sure, there are a lot of retired execs out there who will do this for nothing because they don't need the money. Not the point. The point is, when you pay for something you value you it way more than when it's for free. So structure something that works for you and for them, whether that be cash or stock options in your company. And understand, the more they are involved, the higher the comp should be. If you decide to create an advisory board and you will meet monthly, expect to pay a monthly fee. No matter the level of altruism, good business relationships only work when they are "win-win."

So to take a step back from that tree and observe the forest around you, find that trusted advisor to help you stay that way.

"Advisor, Mentor, Coach. No Matter What They're Called, Results Are All That Matter!"

There is no question that entrepreneurs and small business owners need good advisors. Objective advice is one of the most critical elements in contributing to the success of a small business.

It helps entrepreneurs to avoid the pitfalls and mistakes that the advisor/mentor may have made in their own careers. It further provides objectivity in assisting the small business owner with key decision-making and should help provide a "sounding board" and even a basis for new ideas for the business' success. Yet, with wide variety and availability of advisors, mentors or coaches, how does the small business owner find and use the right advisor for them. And further, what expectations should they have with any advisory relationship?

The right advisor? You may say, "Master Yoda, that sounds like there is some kind of fit for an advisor?" Yes, my aspiring business masters, there is no "one size fits all" advisor. The relationship has to "fit" you and your business. And, above all, you should have some objective in mind, or it can be a very costly and frustrating experience. That's right. Don't just hire an advisor to advise. You can get your Uncle Bert to do that...a lot cheaper. Have some desired results in mind. Whether that be something as simple as more effective decision-making, or better planning techniques or better sales forecasting or assistance with the development of a new product roll-out plan.

So how do find the right one for you?

Experience/Expertise
First and foremost, determine how their experiences and expertise are applicable to you and your business. They don't, necessarily, have to come from your industry sector; while it helps, it's not necessary. But they have to bring something to the table that will help them relate to you and your business. Or, to the business problem or issue you're currently trying to solve. What skills or expertise do they have that you don't? Have they done it themselves, either as experienced entrepreneurs or small business owners, or as advisors to the same type of business as yours (more size or type, like manufacturing, than vertical)? Theory's great, but practical experience is way better!

Chemistry
Second, how's the chemistry between you and the advisor. Important because the old Marshall McLuhan quote, "the medium is the message," applies here. If you have trouble with their personality, style or delivery, you're going to have trouble "hearing" their advice. Get them to give you some free time, where you can see how they work "up close and personal." Make an assessment of them and what you feel they can do for you and your business, before they are actually costing you anything.

Objectives
Third, what do you want them to accomplish and is it realistic? Do you feel confident that they can get it done? Most advisors are mere mortals. They don't work miracles. But if you have a set of objectives in mind, they can, usually tell you if they're rational. Too often, the expectations of a

coaching, mentoring or advisory relationship are "off the chart," way too high on the part of the entrepreneur (or, some circumstances, way oversold by the advisor). Make your objectives realistic, but more important will be whether you feel the advisor can meet them.

Results
At the end of day, however, the only thing that matters are the results delivered. And they shouldn't be "squishy!" If you want cheerleading go to a football game, it's cheaper. If you want somebody to make you feel better about yourself, get a dog. The real measure of an advisor relationship is the positive impact it has on your business and on your operating or management style, that you could not have accomplished alone.

No matter what they're called – advisor, mentor, coach – four things are important – Experience/Expertise, Chemistry, Objectives and Results. But the only one that matters is results!

Chapter 4 – It All Starts with Marketing…

"Know Your Battlefield, Pick Your Battles"

An army going into battle would never think to not understand what the topography of the battlefield was, including critical areas that needed to be captured to ultimately defeat the enemy. They would know where the enemy was entrenched and what resources in manpower and armaments they possessed. Additionally, they would know if they had allied forces in the area, what resources they possessed and how, where and when they might be deployed to help. They would determine where battle lines would be drawn and assaults made and they would continually update that intelligence up to the minute of the assaults and even during battle.

Entrepreneurs are in a business battle every day. Yet, many entrepreneurs don't go into battle with that mindset. Many are using sparse intelligence some of which may not have been updated since they put their original plans together. Most attack every competitive situation without a thought about what the enemy (competition) might do, but only what the business might do to win. Most lack basic information about their enemy like product offerings and pricing and how they compare to the business' offerings and pricing. Few pay enough attention to the tactics that the enemy (competition) uses to win. And typically, they lose more battles than they win because they believe the enemy simply has more resources (both capital and manpower).

And this is further compounded by the fact that the entrepreneurial business is almost always resource-strapped.

So what is a general (the entrepreneur) to do with his rag-tag army up against the well-provisioned enemy that already occupies much of the high ground in the ongoing business battle?

First and foremost, there has to be mindset change.

The entrepreneurial army has to behave like guerilla fighters, picking and choosing what battles to fight. It has to do careful battle planning because of restricted resources. That is, what customers it has the best chance of winning.

As to topography (their target market), they need to better understand what the ideal customer profile is, to better refine that target market and to pick those areas with the best chance of victory, and conversely, with the least enemy resistance (competition). And when a battle is planned, they need to perform extraordinary data gathering about the target customer. They need to know more about the prospective customer than the enemy does and use it to their advantage during the battle (key players, characteristics and attitudes).

Further, they need to know their enemy (competitor(s)), who they are, what they are pitching and pricing and how they sell it in the target market of the ideal customer. Pore over their website. Talk to their own good current customers about what the competitors are presenting (competition is always out there pitching). See if a copy of a proposal that's been submitted can be obtained. Hey, this is war, not a formal dance.

Finally, find allies. Are there companies with whom they can partner, who might already have customer relationships with many of the prospects in the ideal customer profile? Perhaps, they are selling a product that complements the business' product or service. Or perhaps, they can help expand the target market, by carrying the business' product set into that target market. Whatever is done try not to do it alone. A guerilla fighter, can't have too many resources.

In the battle for the customer, know the battlefield, pick the battles, plan the attacks and use all the resources available, inside and outside the company, to win!

It All Starts with Marketing...

"If It Ain't Generating Qualified Leads, Don't Do It!"

For most growing entrepreneurial business, capital resources are always in short supply so smart allocation for their use is critical. Marketing is an area where capital is most frequently wasted. Now I didn't say spending money on marketing is a waste (that is, however, the contention of many "bean-counters" isn't it?) only that it's often not spent wisely. From my experience, the overriding objective of marketing should be to generate qualified leads. No matter how exciting, attractive and ego-stroking your marketing programs might be, if, at the end of the day, they ain't generating qualified leads, you shouldn't be doing them!

Whatever marketing programs you have planned or in place, from your website, to your brochures, to trade shows to advertising, should be judged on their ability to create awareness and interest in your company and its products and/or services.

- Every element should be focused on being "benefits-based," i.e., delivering the message of what your company, products and/or services can do to help address the needs and problems of your prospective customer. Don't just describe features. Describe how they translate into benefits.

- Every element should have a "call to action," that enables prospective customers to learn more about the company, products and/or services. This provides an opportunity to get more information in front of the prospect and then to be able to use that as a springboard to a follow-up call and potential face-to-face meeting. In short, qualified leads.

- Every element should be tracked by the number of qualified leads that come directly or indirectly from it. Every time a prospect interacts with the company, they should be asked where and how they first learned of the company, products and/or services. This will enable you to begin to understand what's working and what has to be changed.

Marketing dollars can be the most cost-effective dollars spent in a small business...but only if they generate qualified leads.

It All Starts with Marketing...

"'First Perceptions' Are Critical... Your Image Can Drive Market Success!"

When it comes to image, perception IS reality. And first "perceptions" are critical. As a small business owner, your company image is formed in a prospect's mind with their first contact, whether it be with your website, your marketing materials, your product pitches or the way your phone is answered. It will make an impression that will get you on the path to making them a customer...or one you may never overcome.

Young companies, especially, need to be aware of this.

Customers want to deal with businesses with whom they are comfortable and confident. That doesn't always mean the largest company in the market, but ones that they want to do business with, feel will best meet and service their needs... and are going to be around for a while to do so! When you're small and struggling, when your resources are few and your confidence not as high as it could be, is when you have to make sure you're not sounding small...or being defensive about being a young company. So what do you do?

Even with limited resources, in today's marketplace, with the low-cost and free tools available, there should be no company that can't create a very professional and exciting first impression.

It starts with your website.
Your website will be the absolute first impression any prospective customer will have of your company. That's where they either discover you or will look when they first hear about you. Make your website as much of a showcase as possible for the brand image you want to create in the market. It should be the centerpiece of all your marketing activities. Use graphics and good copy (get help with this if necessary) to make your company look and sound bigger and more successful than it might be - like a company folks just want to do business with. Now I'm not suggesting being untruthful. However, how you tell your story (highlighting the good parts and not talking about the lesser ones) is what creates your first impression. Make it a lasting one. All marketing materials and product pitches should follow the message you're delivering and the "look and feel" you create on your website. And, make sure that anyone who has any direct contact with a prospect or customer, by phone or in-person, projects the image you're trying to build and delivers the same message.

Social media is important in expanding your image and driving your message.
Establishing a blog can amplify your image by further establishing and building your credibility with both current and prospective customers and should be linked to, or within, your website. Use other social media like Twitter and Facebook to further your image and drive traffic to both your blog and your website. Use a networking service like LinkedIn to help create more awareness of the executives and key players in the company and to help expand your network of potential customers and partners. Cross link all social media.

If first impressions are critical and perception is reality, make the image you create form a lasting first "perception" that turns a prospect into a customer and a customer base into long-term success.

"Being In A Competitive Market Ain't Bad News!"

I've heard so many entrepreneurs lament about the fact that their market has multiple competitors. Contrary to popular belief, that's not the worse news in the world. It means there's actually a market for the product or service you're selling and an opportunity to find a niche for success.

I've also heard folks tell me they have no competition. They're either not paying attention (because if the market is viable, there are competitors out there, they're just disregarding them), or their market niche is infinitesimal or one that nobody else really cares about. Competition is healthy...even when it comes from very large competitors. By their very presence, they give credibility to the market. However, surviving in a competitive market is another thing entirely.

As an entrepreneur, you have to pick and choose your spots. You have to think of yourself as a guerilla warrior, always outmanned and outgunned by larger competition. But that doesn't mean you can't win. It means you can't fight every battle and expect to win. You need to carve out a niche where you can succeed and, in keeping with our military metaphor, "own the high ground."

It All Starts with Marketing...

Typically, in any market, there are segments that are underserved either because the customers are small (but usually numerous) and, therefore, the initial contract value is small, so that for the larger competitors, it's just too inefficient to chase them. This provides an opportunity for the small business to acquire new customers and potentially grow them over time, through upselling. Or it could be that the particular product that you offer is more suited for a particular niche that has been left underserved because only a few competitors have the ability to provide that solution. In any event, if you can find that niche that has sufficient opportunity for you (market size), it will typically have less competition and more chance for success. Conversely, however, trying to play in the competitive mainstream, is often a huge mistake.

A perfect example was a recent client who was a successful niche player in their market. They spent countless hours (and precious resources) to respond to an RFP that represented a huge revenue opportunity with a prospective customer in a market segment where they had no previous success, and therefore no track record. They were up against several much larger competitors, among whom was the current provider, who had both history and track record in that segment. The company felt their success in their niche market segment would translate and good product would win out. Nope and nope!

Not only were they shocked and dismayed by their crushing defeat (finishing near the bottom of more than a half dozen competitors), but it cost them other business, because with limited resources, they couldn't pay sufficient attention to some niche prospects that they ended up also losing. So, it proved to be doubly costly.

Competition is good for the market because it defines it. It also provides a major opportunity for the entrepreneur to find niches in that market that are underserved, for whatever reason. And niches are where entrepreneurs, as guerilla warriors, can best fight their battles, "own the high ground" and the path to long-term success!

It All Starts with Marketing...

"With Limited Resources, Would You Invest in Technology or Marketing?"

If you had already rolled out your product and were faced with making a decision between investing your limited resources in technology to make your product better, or marketing to give your product more visibility, which would you choose?

Always a tough choice. But, the major objective for entrepreneurs, especially in the early going, should be "top line focus" - getting new customers and driving revenue. This revenue should, in turn, drive bottom line, which should then provide the necessary resources to further improve the product.

However, as important, is getting customer feedback on the first iteration of a product to enable ensuing iterations and releases to be as market-driven as possible and limited development resources well-deployed. Too many young companies, especially those that are technology-based, feel the need to constantly improve their product. They use their limited resources to tweak and add features before they've built much of a customer base. Instead, they should be looking to get a base product out there, create and build a solid foundation of customers from whom they can get feedback as to what needs to be changed or be added to the current product to give it broader and deeper appeal.

And the key to creating and building that solid customer foundation and driving revenue is the visibility of the product in the company's target market. In a previous blog post, I noted that "nobody ever bought anything they didn't know about." A young company has to totally focus on creating as much awareness for its product or service to get prospective customers interested in buying it. This is, obviously, marketing. And, with the use of the internet and social media, the resources required to do this are significantly less than they used to be. But it needs to be done, and on a continuous basis, starting with a marketing-driven website as the focal point for any marketing strategy.

Once the company is successfully driving revenue and is getting feedback on its initial product, it could then use both the cash generated and the knowledge gained from its initial customers to develop further enhancements that it can sell back into its existing customer base and to new customers. And the process continues.

Given the choice of deployment of limited resources, always pick revenue and customers before product enhancement. Once you have the former, the latter becomes way easier to achieve.

It All Starts with Marketing...

"Want to Sell More Customers? Make It About Them!"

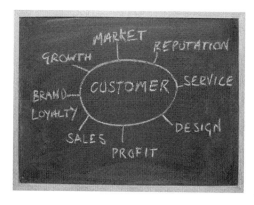

Such a simple concept, but so hard for entrepreneurs and small business owners, so passionate about their product or service, to understand. Instead of focusing their marketing message on the need their product or service fills or the problem it solves, many entrepreneurs want to tell prospective customers about every conceivable feature and function. So, they overwhelm the customer message with buzzwords and industry jargon and the answer to the critical customer question – "what can this do for me?" gets lost.

Recently, one of my small business clients introduced a major product innovation to their market. Now, they were a relatively small, entrepreneurial, niche player, with a deep technology focus and had really not done much in the way of marketing, prior to this product launch. But their new product was a "game changer," both for them, and more importantly, for their customers.

They planned a major campaign, using various types of marketing from a website upgrade to email to p.r. to social media. However, the closer they got to the ultimate kickoff, the more focused their message on the technology (their comfort zone) as opposed to the product benefits (the customer's comfort zone). The result? Lots of interest, but more questions than answers from their customers. And more important, a very slow uptake on new orders as the marketplace better understand what was in it for them!

Are you doing similar things in your business? Look at the messages you are sending out to your customers. Is your website (beyond your About section) all about how great you and your products/services are? Or is about how you can fill multiple customer needs or solve multiple customer problems?

Do email campaigns focus on getting customers to act because it's good for them (for example, a trial use of your product aimed at addressing a particular need) or because it's good for you (try out our award-winning product)?

Is your product literature simply a litany of every possible feature and function, screaming out – "ain't we great?" Instead it should be screaming out "ain't we great…for you?"

Ultimately, business success is predicated on how well entrepreneurs address a customer need or solve a customer problem, answering the customer question – "what's in it, for me?" The marketing message you send to the customer begins that success…or not. At the end of the day, entrepreneurial success is always about the customer.

It All Starts with Marketing...

"'Happy Birthday from ABC Ford' – Good Plan, Crummy Execution"

Just the other day, I got this really nice email from an auto dealer from whom I had leased or purchased several vehicles in the past. It said simply in the subject line – Happy Birthday from ABC Ford (I have substituted ABC for their name to protect the guilty). And in the body of the email "my friends from ABC" wished me a happy birthday and presented me with a birthday service special for my Ford Expedition, which they hoped I was enjoying. Two problems with that. First, it wasn't my birthday (same day, wrong month). Second, even worse, I haven't owned an Expedition in more than three years.

So what could have been a very thoughtful way to both re-affirm a relationship with a customer and build on that relationship with a discounted service, only left me shaking my head. Their lack of up-to-date customer data turned an attempt at a good customer service advance into just making them look dumb. If they couldn't even establish that I was still a customer or what my birthday was (both of which they had at one time), how "buttoned up" could the management of their dealership be? A good customer service plan scuttled by poor execution. A positive turned into a negative.

And how often have we seen this situation? Probably, way more times than we care to even think about. And it is so avoidable!

Usually, even within a small company it's a right hand not knowing what the left hand is doing. Where marketing puts a good direct marketing plan together only to have the IT guy drop the ball by providing an old data base for the direct marketing. Or worse, marketing not even asking IT for the right database, but just using one that they had had for a while, assuming it was correct.

And what is the takeaway from this?

Customer-facing functions like marketing and customer service are not functions that should exist on their own. They need other functions in the company to support their efforts. But, even more important, since they are functions that interact directly with prospects and customers, they are the lifeblood of a company's present and future revenue streams. In fact, anything that involves customers, especially, should be a company-wide responsibility with ownership by every function. And finally, communication within the organization is essential. Plans should be shared, support should be sought, so that the company comes across in the best possible light with customers and achieves whatever objectives the program had.

Take my situation. If they had planned to contact old customers, wishing them a happy birthday would have been a very thoughtful and impressive thing. Including an invitation for a test drive of a brand new vehicle (maybe like one I had purchased in the past) or, a special leasing deal to "get me back," would have been a great program and might have actually gotten my attention. However, clearly, it was aimed at "existing" customers, with the special servicing deal. So it was a double loss. It went to a wrong or old database with the wrong offer. All those precious marketing dollars...wasted. And it could have been avoided.

It All Starts with Marketing…

Creating good marketing and customer service plans and programs are necessary for a small business to grow and succeed. Company-wide ownership of them and their execution should be the basis for that success.

Chapter 5 – It Ends with Sales. Without Sales, There is No Business!

"Do You Sleep with Your Sales Forecast Under Your Pillow?"

If I've heard it once, I've heard it a thousand times from small business owners – "the biggest problem with our sales is that we don't have enough leads in our forecast."

Usually, in my own flip way, I tell them I can help that. Get me the yellow pages... you get the picture. It isn't how many leads are in the pipeline, it's how many **qualified leads** are in the pipeline!

But it just appears that some folks get some level of comfort in seeing $xx thousands or millions of potential sales in a forecast. Kind of sleep with it under their pillow to make them feel better, when if they truly understood what a good sales forecast was, they'd be having nightmares!

Sales forecasts are one of the most important elements in a company's success...and one of the most misunderstood.

First of all, it is, above all else, a forecast. In short, what is projected vs. what will actually happen? Second, its credibility is not dependent on how large the potential dollars from a sale, but on the confidence that some portion of the potential dollars will actually arrive in the form of new sales and can be counted on, over time. And that credibility is seated in two things – how qualified the leads or prospects are, and what the conversion rate of those qualified leads has been over time.

Let's address each in turn.

Now the old sales adage is "leads = sales." That is the more leads you have, the more sales you close. Sounds reasonable, right? Nope. Only partially right. It's, actually, the more *qualified leads* you have, the more sales you close.

Qualified leads, basically, come from the various marketing programs the company has instituted. At the end of day, marketing's major, if not only, objective is to generate qualified leads. The difference between a lead and a qualified lead? A lead is "aware," but a qualified lead is "aware" and "interested." Most marketing programs are established to create awareness. Not enough focus on getting potential prospects "interested."

Some examples of "interested" leads are those who don't just visit a website, but opt-in for a download, newsletter or blog. Or they could be prospects with whom a demonstration has been scheduled as the result of some kind of marketing program. Those are the only prospects that ought to appear on a forecast. If they haven't exhibited interest, then they are just a suspect, and although they still might be pursued, they should not be counted in any way. A forecast or pipeline only contains qualified leads. They can't be closed if they aren't, at least, interested. Check your latest forecast. How many of the prospects shown are truly qualified?

The conversion rate, determined over time is the % of qualified leads that, ultimately, are closed. And this is really the true measure of how good a sales force is performing. This is a direct result of a good sales process, a step-by-step way to take a qualified lead from "interested" to "customer."

The better the sales process, the higher the conversion rate. Just because a qualified lead appears on a forecast does not make it a "take it to the bank" situation. Do you know what your conversion rate is? And how good is your sales process? Time to review what it takes to move a qualified lead from "interested" to "closed."

So, a forecast is only as good as the *qualified leads* that comprise it and the conversion rates that turn those leads into actual sales. A forecast built and managed in this way, won't guarantee your success or a good night's sleep, but won't give you nightmares, either!

It Ends with Sales. Without Sales, There is No Business!

"Do You Lead with Price...Leaving Money on the Table and Losing Potential Customers in the Process?"

There have been countless small business owners that I have spoken to and advised, whose nearly first comment, as they describe their business, is how low-priced their product or service is. Now being the low-priced provider is one thing, but making price your leading advantage is again another... and not a good one! How you price and how you use price are critically important to a small business, especially when you are competing against much larger competitors.

Knowing the cost of delivering your product or service (not just cost of goods sold, but also what it costs to sell and support it) is absolutely critical to establishing a price at which you can make money. Most often a small company can price itself under most or all of its larger competitors, carrying less overhead, having a lower cost base, etc., but it needs to be sure it understands its cost vs. its price and is generating margins it can live and grow with. And that needs to be reviewed periodically.

I had a client that was so proud that they had not raised their prices in more than ten years. When I asked them if they had given out any raises during that time or if the cost of materials and services to deliver their product had increased they looked at me like "a deer in the headlights."

Oops... never thought of that! No good having the lowest price if you aren't making money at it.

Too many small companies make the mistake of figuring that leading with price will win the day, often lowering an already low price to ensure success. Shaving margins, leaving money on the table and maybe, ultimately, still not winning the business. Like the old saying, "if your only tool is a hammer, every problem is a nail." They focus so completely on price, and a lower price at that, that it raises questions in the minds of the prospective customer if they are getting lower price because your product or service is of less quality or depth.

Price is only one of the key elements necessary for successfully selling a product or service. Obviously, a given is that no matter how low-priced your product is, if it doesn't meet market and potential customer requirements, and isn't of high quality, you won't sell very much. But beyond the obvious, is how you deliver and support that product or service.

This is often where the small business can really show and provide its difference. The care with which you and your employees develop and deliver your product or service and the extent to which you support and service it, are as critical, if not more so, than pricing. Plus, the small company can and will be more customer-attentive, providing service levels that the larger company competitors often cannot compete with. Tie this to your price. You're not just lower priced, but more cost-effective for your customer. In short, they get more, for less!

Don't lead with price. Let price speak for itself. After you've convinced them that your product or service is a high

It Ends with Sales. Without Sales, There is No Business!

quality one that more than meets their requirements, show them (especially through current customer references) that the service and support level that they will get with it will surpass their wildest expectations. Then your price makes a difference!

"Are the Results of Your Chasing 'Big Wins' Just a Closet Full of Pastel-Colored Dresses?"

For some small businesses there are no sales opportunities, especially ones with the potential to bring the "big win," that they won't chase. The lure of it is just too much to turn away from. Many entrepreneurs chase the "big win" in hopes that it will either "put the company on the map" or "make it well." It's almost intoxicating. Or, more often, wishing and hoping! For few small businesses find consistent success in constantly going after the "big win." Many finish second (or worse), behind bigger, stronger, more experienced competitors.

"Always a bridesmaid, never a bride," that frustrating description of always getting close to winning the big prize, but never quite getting there, can be a devastating strategy.

In business, often like in life, finishing second usually means getting nothing but a "consolation prize." The literal version was a movie, "Bridesmaid," where the main character, lamented over her closet full of pastel-colored dresses. Unfortunately, many small businesses get the figurative version of that. They end up feeling good about how they got "so close," but, nonetheless, lost to either a bigger or better competitor. And in the process wasted precious resources and time that could have been dedicated to going after and closing smaller, oftentimes, more profitable deals.

It Ends with Sales. Without Sales, There is No Business!

Now this doesn't mean entrepreneurs shouldn't chase after the "big win." It just needs to be done in a very measured way, by developing a sales strategy that neither depends on "big wins" nor eliminates chasing them.

But how can that strategy ensure that you don't become "the best second place team?" Here are four steps to avoid having "a closet full of pastel-colored dresses:"

Pick and Choose Your Battles
With always limited resources, small business owners cannot afford to respond to every opportunity. Further, entrepreneurs can't continually pursue these "big win" kind of opportunities as a normal course of business. Pick and choose the situations where you chase; where you have the best opportunity to succeed. Maybe, less competition, maybe the size or type of customer that defines your business' "sweet spot." Whatever your criteria, it should be to increase your odds of winning.

Prepare...but be Prepared to Back Out
Preparation is always critical, especially in understanding as much about the situation as possible. For example, if you're asked to bid on an RFP and the functional requirements/questions appear to be very specifically-focused around key functions of a competitive product offering, it might very well be that the deck is already stacked to their advantage. Especially, if that supplier is the incumbent in the situation. This one has "bridesmaid" written all over it. So knowing when to fold is equally important. Saves you resources, time and aggravation, later.

Develop a Unique Approach/Solution
If you're one of the smaller, if not the smallest player in this "big win" situation, in order to get noticed and to increase your odds of winning, entrepreneurs have to try to "change

the rules!" Obviously, it's a given that you want what your small business promises to be viewed as better, more valuable, more cost-effective, etc.

However, try to present your proposal in the most unique way possible, where it would be difficult for your prospective customer to completely compare apples to apples, be it through packaging (maybe providing "all-in" features/functions) or pricing (subscription vs. one-time purchase) as opposed to the typical a la carte way that most companies bid. And this can be done, even when responding to an RFP. Whatever you do, make it stand out, so they have to look deeper.

Learn and Grow
And finally, win or lose, learn from the situation. If you win, find out from your new customer, what drove their decision and build on it in future, comparative deals. If you lose, ask the prospect for a post-mortem meeting, or at worst case, a telephone call, to better understand what you could have done differently to have won. If there was nothing different you could have done except to have been a bigger company (and that happens, as you know, way more than you'd like to think) then you know that, in the future, these are not the kind of opportunities to go after...unless or until you get bigger!

The lure of the "big win," especially for entrepreneurs with small struggling companies, can sometimes be too great to avoid. Approach with caution. There is no consolation prize, no revenue, when your small business finishes second!

It Ends with Sales. Without Sales, There is No Business!

"Is Your Sales and Marketing Strategy Simply SATW?"

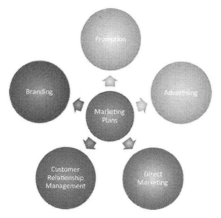

Does your small business have a real sales and marketing strategy? One that, specifically, defines your target market, that sets out specific strategies and tactics (and budgets) to penetrate those markets. One that generates qualified leads/prospects, for your small business, that can be closed?

Or is your sales and marketing strategy, like so many other small businesses today, one of indiscriminately chasing every opportunity that comes at you, every potential prospect, no matter how remote the potential of close? Is your strategy simply SATW? That is, do you just "throw stuff against the wall" and hope something sticks?

Is this you? Is this your approach to small business sales and marketing? If it is, know that you're not alone and there's a reason for it...and a way to fix it.

Sales in the early going of a small business startup are crucial to not only its success, but its very viability. Entrepreneurs learn early that you need prospects to create sales so they chase as many of them as possible. Often the entrepreneur will do anything and everything to get those early sales, rarely turning away a prospect, regardless how remote the probability for success. Even as the company matures and grows, this early model, which enabled survival becomes more and more difficult to abandon, and after a while becomes the de facto sales and marketing strategy for this small business.

And it's insidious. Some entrepreneurs don't even realize it...until they wake up one morning and they're no further along this year than they were last year...or the year before. And the essence of sales growth is to have a marketing strategy that generates qualified leads/prospects that can be closed.

Here are the telltale signs and what you can do to counteract them and develop a real focused strategy for your small business:

"Looking for Love in all the (Wrong) Places"
Your market niche is anything moving in your overall target market. You make no distinction as to whether you have a chance to close a situation, only that you need to chase it. If RFPs guide your market, you respond to all of them, even if the incumbent is ten times your size and can outman and outgun you.

> *What to do* – Be a guerrilla fighter, not only picking and choosing where to battle, but target your battles in the niches where you have had the most success, and maybe where the competition is less intense. Build future success on the past and present successes you've had and try to "own" a market segment niche.

"All Things to All People"
You have no marketing plan. Your marketing tactics are either totally focused on one medium (like trade shows) or so diffused that you're doing a different thing every week (email blasts, trade advertising, direct mail, etc.), without any kind of plan, in hopes that something will hit. Worse,

It Ends with Sales. Without Sales, There is No Business!

you really don't track what success you may or may not have with any one tactic.

> *What to do* – Once again, understand what your niche market is and determine how to best reach that audience and then tailor your tactics accordingly. If that audience regularly attends three trade shows, so should you. If they are too widely distributed for advertising, seek more targeted marketing like email or direct mail. And whatever you do, track your sales and marketing strategy tactics' success in generating qualified leads/prospects.

"Social Media is Just a Fad (or the Only Important Tool)"
Being extreme is never a good thing. Social media should not be ignored, nor is it the "be all, end all." Blogging every day or constant updates to Facebook are only important if they have some kind of objective behind them, especially in advancing your brand or image in your targeted niche. Not considering social media important can create a positioning for your brand or image whether you like it or not.

> *What to do* – Create a manageable sales and marketing Strategy for a social media campaign aimed at providing you more visibility within your overall market and your targeted niche. Make sure "your voice" (the image you want to create for your company) is evident and consistent in everything you do.

Sales and marketing are inextricably tied together. But without a focused marketing strategy that generates qualified leads/prospects, there can be no sales. And a marketing strategy that has no focus will generate leads, but not necessarily ones that can be closed.

SATW doesn't work as a strategy for your sales and marketing. Get focused. Get a plan. Gain the success you're after.

Chapter 6 – Love and Support Your Customer!

"Are You Making It Easy for Customers to Do Business With You?"

Obviously, small business success begins and ends with the customer. Especially in difficult economic times like these, every qualified prospect is a potential customer and every current customer has the potential for more sales, and should be viewed as "precious gold" to the entrepreneur's business. Yet many small companies, as their success brings growth beyond "every customer on a first name basis" stage, unwittingly, make it extra difficult for prospective or even current customers to do business with them. And it's so easy to overlook some very obvious signs. Here are some key questions to ask yourself regarding how your company treats prospective and current customers:

- When's the last time you reviewed how all of your "customer facing" functions interact with your prospects or customers? Not just sales and marketing or customer service, but billing (and collections!), your website, right down to how your phone gets answered and what's on your voice mail message?

- How easy is it for customers to get samples or test your product? While no product sells itself, your chances sure improve if a prospect can get to see how your product performs, "up close and personal." So, make it as easy as possible to get your products into a prospective customer's hands.

- Do you take current, long-time customers for granted by not providing your customer service people with up-to-date information about the customer and their account when they call in? Nothing frustrates a long-time (or high volume) customer more than not being acknowledged as "special."

- Do you track how often a company representative (officer, sales person, account manager/field support, etc., calls on current customers? Current customers still remain the best and shortest-term opportunity for new and additional sales. Are you capitalizing on or ignoring this opportunity?

- Is your website customer friendly, or so chock full of technical wizardry that only the most technically competent prospects or customers can navigate it? When's the last time you tried to use it and with what success? The owner/CEO test is almost always the best one.

- If you sell through e-commerce on your website, do you track how often and why prospective customers leave the website without buying, even though they put items in their cart? Perhaps, in your concern with security you're making it really hard for them to pay you.

These are just a few of the key things to consider in order to ensure that your company is "customer-friendly," and is creating the environment for additional business success.

"In a Small Business, Building a Customer Base is the Lifeblood of Success...and Everybody Has a Role, Including the Customer!"

Most folks know how important revenue is to the success of a small business. That's why the sales function is so critical in the early going. But few small business owners understand how important building and maintaining the customer base, responsible for that revenue, really is. And, that it should be the number one objective of every single person in the company.

But while most small businesses are focused on the sales they generate, few focus enough on the customer base that represents those sales. It is the customer base that is the lifeblood of the company's future success. The relationship you build with that base is how you grow...or not.

That said, what are the key elements that you, the entrepreneur, need to consider in building and growing a customer base?

A Customer Today is Success Tomorrow

While the customer is a source of revenue from their initial purchase, often, their major potential is for additional revenue from new sales in the future. It's way easier and more profitable to sell into an existing customer situation than develop a new one. So that customer relationship can almost be viewed as a distribution channel for future revenue. And it depends, exclusively, on how well that relationship is nurtured.

It's a Team Effort

In a small business, getting a new customer often involves several functions within the company beyond just sales. Depending on the product or service, somebody has to deliver it. Accounting has to bill for it (and, of course, collect). Customer service or the help desk has to support it. And so on. But do each of these functional areas understand their role in the sale? That when the customer buys the company's product or service, they are "buying" the company that underpins that product or service...or they wouldn't buy? All employees should be aware that they are part of a team in supporting a sale to a customer and get them to embrace their role.

The Personal Touch

Every prospective or current customer wants and expects a live, friendly person ready to help them when they call you. The first voice they hear, whether it's the first time they call or the hundredth time should represent how you want your company presented. While it's more efficient, hearing some "by rote" greeting from an automated answering system ain't exactly providing a good first impression. But that's where the building a customer base begins.

Maniacally Responsive

Once the customer is on board, how well their needs or requirements, after the sale, are addressed predicts the likelihood they will remain a customer and purchase additional products or services from the company. And they, too, are important in building the customer base of which they are a part, because if they are happy, they tell other potential customers about their experience with your company.

How responsive is your company to your customers? Ever try posing as a customer, calling either the main telephone number or customer service five minutes before you open or five minutes before you close with an urgent request? Or an order? Every call from a customer or prospect should be treated like it's potential revenue, with every employee focused on going "the extra mile."

Partner vs. Vendor
Do you collaborate with customers? Do you truly listen to them? Do they consider you a partner or a simply another vendor? Are you a trusted advisor or still bidding on jobs as they come up? Are you inside their decision-making circle, or outside waiting for a call as to your fate?

And, internally, are customers viewed as simply a bother? Does your staff have the old railroad mentality – "we could run this railroad better if it wasn't for all these customers?" Help them understand, the customer base pays their salaries.

Social Media as "the Voice of the Company"
Use social media not only to make connections to new prospects, but to create "your voice" within your customer base. Whatever you use, Facebook, Twitter, LinkedIn, etc., post messages that are of value to your customer and prospect base and consistently drive home how you want your company perceived. Make sure you, as the owner, have a hand in or author a lot of those messages. Your company should have your voice.

Generating revenue is important to the success of any small business. But building the customer base from that revenue

Love and Support Your Customer!

is the key to that success, long-term...and it should be the #1 objective of everybody in the company!

"A Good Customer Relationship is Built on Appreciation and Begins with 'Thank You!'"

Do you ever thank your customer for the sale? The focus in, virtually, every small business is new customer acquisition. Every entrepreneur takes great pains to make sure that they do everything possible to close a sale and get a new customer. Yet, when the order is placed, at the very moment that the relationship begins, there's an opportunity to reinforce the sale with a simple "thank you." A small gesture, yet one that starts the relationship as a two-way one and begins the foundation for a long-term one.

And does your customer feel appreciated well after that sale? Appreciation is the fundamental foundation upon which entrepreneurs should build all customer relationships.

And it mostly just inolves little things.

To start with, once the sale is closed, send the new customer, a nice letter, a friendly email or even a personal call from the small business owner. Internally, a recognition and celebration of the new customer and, depending on your revenue model, an onboarding plan, not unlike that for a

Love and Support Your Customer!

new employee. (Obviously, the higher your average ticket price, the more important and possible this becomes).

The entrepreneur should use every "touch point" to show the customer you care, including your packaging. Ever get a shipment from Zappo's? It has two phrases on the outside of the box - "packaged with happiness" and "charged with service." Now, that gets a customer's attention!

And, of course, along the way, you provide good customer support. But, to show ongoing appreciation, your small business should implement outgoing communications from customer support - a "reach out" program to, periodically, determine, as the former mayor of New York, Ed Koch, used to ask, "how am I doing?"

Every customer should feel special, not just before, but during, after and well after the initial sale! Appreciation is the fundamental foundation upon which entrepreneurs should build all customer relationships with their small business. And it begins with "thank you!"

"Customer Service...The Choice for Growth!"

There's no getting around it. While every company starts out with zero revenue, whether you grow to $100,000 in annual revenue or $100 million, is by and large *your choice*.

Now I can already hear the naysayers among you, "But Master Yoda, it's not that simple. Sometimes, the market is against you. Or sometimes you don't have enough capital, blah, blah, blah."

Nope. Usually, what keeps you from growing your business to where you want it to grow comes down to the choices you make in a key area.

Most companies that don't grow very big do so by choice, some conscious, most not. And, make no mistake, big growth is not essential for everyone. Creating a lifestyle business that limits growth to owner-bandwidth or lifestyle factors is a choice. But for this posting, it's the businesses that want to grow but don't, also out of choice, sometimes even subconscious, are what I'm focused on.

Sales is the foundation of business growth, but is followed very closely by customer service. Just so we're on the same page, my definition of customer service is building and maintaining customer relationships (the C-R of CRM). It is

Love and Support Your Customer!

not just a function, but a culture of making every customer feel like they are your only customer; creating a bond, a long-term relationship, whether they are your biggest or your smallest. Many entrepreneurs will give it "lip service," but, given the economic choice, don't think customer service is THAT important.

If I polled a thousand people in business, and asked what are the two biggest factors in growing a business, sales might get mentioned more than half the time, good product 75-80%, but customer service, actually building and maintaining customer relationships, might not even get 10%. Of course, capital would be right there at the top.

There is no dispute regarding the importance of top line to every business success. But it is customer service, as defined above, that actually helps fuel sales growth. It is, most often, the prime contact point for customers once the initial sale has been completed, making them feel "loved" by the company through being responsive to their needs, addressing their questions and reacting to their issues, helping create a long-term relationship.

Providing good customer service to existing customers is the major basis for satisfied customers and repeat sales. Satisfied customers create customer references and customer references bring new sales from other new customers. But invariably, the customer service function is overlooked or ignored, or worse, actually de-emphasized, and most often, by choice, often driven from previous experience.

Fortunately or unfortunately, we are products of our experience and our environment. Most entrepreneurs had their initial training and exposure to business in large companies. And what has been the most disturbing trend in large companies over the past ten years or so is the outsourcing of customer service. That is, sending a prime customer-facing function to another country that may not even have the same primary language - all in the interest of cost-savings. It is a major example of being penny-wise and pound foolish! Costs much less...and most companies, who've done it, get what they pay for in poor customer service, not realizing how much it is really costing in lost sales.

And so, when the bright young entrepreneur finally ventures out on his/her own, starting up a business, the message remembered is the one delivered to them in their formative business years – customer service is a commodity service where you keep labor costs as low as possible.

I am, often, called in by young companies who had begun growing their top line very nicely, only to have sales stall or worse, just fall off dramatically. And when I dig just a little, typically, I find they've made a bad choice. For reasons they justify as economic, they usually have a customer service function that is so undermanned and overworked that it's almost as bad as having no customer service function at all. Or worse, neither has the function been staffed nor is the culture of customer service anywhere in existence. Once the sale is completed, the customer relationship becomes "catch as catch can." This usually results in a less than happy customer base and a whole bunch of lost opportunity.

Small business owners, as I've already noted in previous blog postings, sales is everybody's job. But to fuel growth, learn to love your customers, creating a bond with them from the CEO right on down to the person who answers the phone. Customer service is also everybody's job. For growth, it's your choice!

Chapter 7 – Building a Successful Organization is about the Culture You Create and How You Treat Employees

"The Culture You Create Is the Soul of Your Enterprise!"

When an entrepreneur starts a business, probably the last thing they think about is the culture they are going to create within it. Yet, it is probably the most powerful force that, later, drives the company forward...or not.

The business concept, the underlying technology, the great idea are usually what becomes the underpinning foundation that births the business. But, once all this migrates from the founder(s) to its first employee(s) is truly when it becomes a business...and when the actual DNA of the business is established. Its soul!

As I've noted in other postings, we are a product of our environment. As our parents raised us is often how we establish how we live our lives, raise our children. Just as often, our early jobs set the stage for how we behave in business. We, often, manage as we have been managed. And with the way companies churn through people and the way B-schools continue their heavy focus on process rather than combination of process and intuition, we are ending up with more and more managers who feel that people are a necessary evil to a business. Mere cogs in the machine! And that often gets translated to a bad end, when these same managers endeavor to become entrepreneurs.

I'll never forget my first entrepreneurial or, I guess before it became fashionable, "intrapreneurial" business. I was barely

Building a Successful Organization

27 years old and running an IT company that I had started for a major conglomerate. One day, early on, it dawned on me, that every major decision I made was setting policy for the company, Every action I was taking was being viewed by the employees as the way we should behave as an organization. I was, literally crafting a culture. Only years later, when I started my first business with my own money, did I really understand that I had the opportunity to create a company that not only made money, but stood for something. My values.

And this is what every entrepreneur faces at some point in time or another. They are creating the culture of their business with every decision they make, every day that they are in business. They are setting the tone for the values the company will espouse. But just as often, they are ill-prepared from an experiential viewpoint to create an environment that is conducive to personal and professional growth for its people, which ALWAYS translates into growth for the company. The biggest result of how you treat your people will be reflected in how your people treat your customers. If they're working in a setting where it's fun to work, they are respected, trusted and challenged and made to feel proud to be a part of it, your customers will see that in every interaction. And the company will thrive. Unfortunately, the opposite is also true, however, the company usually doesn't see it until it's too late and it's heading south.

The culture of your enterprise can simply happen as the result of how the business evolves or you can be proactive in crafting it. Look at it as the "soul" of your enterprise. It should reflect the values of the owner(s) and/or the vision of the kind of company the owner(s) want to create. Like most things, there are no right answers for what that should be, but here are some thoughts.

If you haven't had good example of a company you admire in your past, find a model you like. I was fortunate. In my first job, I worked for IBM, back in the day when their guiding principle was "respect for the individual." It was a hugely paternalistic organization with well stated and well-practiced values and the employee loyalty that the company engendered was incredible. That made such an impression on me, that it drove the way decisions were made and employees managed for years after.

Unfortunately, not everyone starts out with that kind of good base. But there are plenty of good examples out there. Read about good companies, good models. But don't just copy one. What works for one company won't necessarily work for another. Think about the environment you want to create for you and your people. Pick and choose what works for you.

A couple of key things you should think about:

- Build your company on a foundation of trust and mutual respect, where teamwork is encouraged over individual endeavors. Make it a fun place to work. Now that doesn't mean you have to have a foosball table in the middle of the office or Friday afternoon beer parties, but it does mean that you keep humor and levity as part of the fabric of the company, challenge your people to grow and create opportunities for socializing with peers.

- Hold people accountable. Make them responsible for their actions. Allow them to take risks, but don't fire them if they fail. Mixed messages!

Building a Successful Organization

- Above all, keep communicating. Keep them informed...of progress, or even the lack of it. If they feel part of the team, they will have your back in tough times.

- Finally, make them a part of ownership of the company, wherever possible. Using stock options as a way to incentivize employees and create more a feeling of participation can increase employee pride (this is MY company) and increase the company's value, because everybody is working toward the same end.

These are just some ideas. However, whatever you create, write it down, make it something employees can carry around with them, have it at their desk, or even give to customers, so everybody knows what the company stands for.

I ran a major division for a public company, years back that had a mantra of "hustle," even a poem written by the CEO. Yeah, a little hokey, but we all carried these plastic cards, that not only had the poem on one side, but on the other side our mission and key objectives – which really defined our values. You know, that culture was so embedded in me, that twenty plus years later, I still carry that card!

The culture of a company is its soul. Create and develop it wisely. It will pay extraordinary dividends.

Secrets to Entrepreneurial Success

"Celebrate Small Victories!"

Choosing to be an entrepreneur means you believed enough in yourself and your business concept to risk the security of a regular job, a regular paycheck. It gave you the opportunity to "live life on the fault line," as your business got launched and haltingly began to generate revenue, and maybe even some positive cash flow. Every major step forward was a small victory to be celebrated. You know the ones. Like your first customer. Your first good review by some industry press. Your first major contract. Did you allow yourself to celebrate them?

Small victories are what it takes to drive success. Sure we'd all love to have that big, earth-shattering victory, that win of a huge proposal over a half dozen other competitors or that industry recognition award that puts you in "elite" category in your sector. But, by and large, it's that small contract win, that customer endorsement or that new customer account that helps your company grown, year in and year out. To use an analogy from my avocation, baseball, where I coached for more than 30 years, it's playing for one run – "small ball" vs. waiting for the three-run homerun to win the game. While I'd love the big hit, I'll take the sure run, every time.

But it's not just understanding the importance of small victories; it's celebrating them that's equally important.

Now, as your small business has slowly grown, maybe even added a bunch of employees, do you still celebrate small victories? While today's might pale in comparison with those of the "early days," in importance to the overall success of the company, they're still important, especially, to key employees or customers (yes, you can and should celebrate customer "victories").

If you don't acknowledge and celebrate small victories, or maybe even never have, you should think about it as part of the culture you're continually creating for your small business. It provides the opportunity to recognize what individual or team achievement means to the company's success. The first sale by your newest account rep. The first defect-free delivery month for your new production guy. Or your development team delivering the new release, on time and bug-free (well, maybe not such a small victory).

It can also help you in solidifying the bond between your company and your customers by recognizing some of their achievements (whether or not you had a part in them). Like one of your customer's 100th year in business. Or, the CEO of one of your customers getting a big Chamber of Commerce award. Or one of your customers being able to reduce their product cost due to a part you made for them, more cost-effectively.

And none of it has to be a big deal.

People, no matter, whom or where, want to be recognized for their efforts. Celebrating small victories does that. Whether it's a pizza lunch, a plaque, flowers, a donation to a charity, no matter. Recognize them, both the small victories and those responsible, both inside your company and with your customers, and they will pay huge dividends to your success.

"Hiring the Right People...and Holding them Accountable Is Critical to Growing Your Business!"

One of the most difficult transitions an entrepreneur faces is going from "the garage" to a real business, from "getting by" to generating real and sustaining revenue. And the most difficult part of that transition is hiring and managing employees who will help deliver that revenue and make future growth possible. The challenges of this major step often make the challenges of getting the business off the ground seem like a "walk in the park."

Now, I'm assuming that you've already been through the outsource versus in-house decision, so we'll proceed on the premise that you've decided to hire rather than contract. But once you decide you will be hiring, then you face a series of critical questions – what positions to hire for, how to hire, who to hire and how to manage them? – that can often determine how well, or if, you can grow your business.

Hire to replace you.
Initially, hire for positions that will take a majority of either the labor-intensive work or required functions for which you are not strong (e.g. marketing, where your strength might be development) from your shoulders.

Building a Successful Organization

Define the position.
As best you can, define what you want from the position, including type of background or experience you'd like to have; responsibilities the job entails and proposed compensation you're willing to pay. Use your advisors and close colleagues to help you create this. As to where to find the folks you're looking for, before you go to a resume mill (e.g., Monster, CareerBuilder, Ladders, etc.), use your network. They know you best and will often recommend people to you who they think are a good match. If that fails (and even if it doesn't) post the job on the various sites. You can't have enough good candidates to screen.

Hire the right people.
Easier said than done! When interviewing, look for folks that fit within the culture you've developed or are developing. Tony Hsieh of the famed Zappo's had a good rule of thumb for their early (and even later) hires - "people we'd like to hang out with." Obviously, they have to have the skill sets required for the job, but hiring people who you would like to work with can't hurt. (As for interviewing skills that few of us have, I'd recommend you take a look at Carol Quinn's website - www.hireauthority.com where she has a short course that you can secure to help you find the best potential performers for a job.)

Put people in a position where they can succeed.
To do that they need to have the right background and skills for the job. Then, they need to be properly trained for the position. If you know exactly how the job should be performed (since you were probably the one who was doing it) don't just show them, train them, through repetition and feedback. Specifically define the responsibilities of their job and expectations for their performance. Then give them the authority to carry out those responsibilities - i.e., give them

the ability to make fundamental decisions. And critical to this last point, allow them to make mistakes...we all do... without the threat of firing. Having them learn from those mistakes (so long as they don't keep making the same ones over and over – then you have problem) is a way, both, for, them to grow personally and professionally, and for the position to continually be better defined and expanded, as necessary.

Hold them accountable.
Whoever you hire, hold them accountable for the responsibilities and expectations you've defined. Since they are in control (they have the authority to carry out those responsibilities), encourage their "ownership" of their job. Once they establish ownership, accountability is a "no-brainer." And accountability is the key to not only getting the job done, but getting it done well.

Hiring the right folks for the right positions, then having them take ownership of those positions and holding them accountable for the responsibilities and expectations associated can become the foundation for success and future growth of a small business.

Building a Successful Organization

"People - Engaging and Motivating Them Is One of the Keys to Small Business Success!"

Since I've managed, grown and done turnarounds across multiple industries, many folks have asked me, especially in the turnaround situations how I was able to come in and quickly transition into such disparate businesses and operations. I turn the questions right back at them and say "what is the common denominator across all businesses?"

It's people!

People who are employees. People who are customers. People who are suppliers. And the relationships we build with each of them.

Back nearly 40 years ago, in his seminal work, Megatrends, author John Naisbitt coined the phrase, "high tech, high touch," describing that in a world of high technology, people still wanted and appreciated personal, human contact. And in our, increasingly, virtual world, we may be overlooking this critical aspect of business success.

How well you engage and motivate the people who interact with your business will, for the most part, determine how successful you will be.

Keeping all your employees, whether you have two or twenty-two, engaged and motivated by keeping them constantly informed about where the business is, what the plans are for it, how important each of them is to it and what their role is in its potential success, provides a critical foundation piece for that success. Even if you are a virtual company, have periodic face-to-face meetings. It will go a long way into everyone feeling a part of something bigger than their "little corner of the world."

Except for commodity products, easily purchased via the internet, people still buy from people. Even in the commodity situation, while price will play a major role, how well the website engages the customer, makes it easy for them to use it and order the product, will often be the difference between a sale and not.

Same thing applies on a larger scale to a major product or consultative sale. The more you know, engage and motivate your prospect with first, understanding their business; and second, how the benefits of your product or service meet the needs of that business, the more comfortable that prospect will feel about your company and the more successful you will be. And, back to employees, the more engaged they are, the more they will engage customers when they call for support or questions, further solidifying the customer relationship.

And finally, with key suppliers, just because you are a very small portion of a supplier's business does not mean that you shouldn't create a solid relationship with them from the "get-go," especially, if they are also a small business. Set up a meeting with their CEO and tell them about your company, your goals and plans and how important the relationship with them will be to your company's success. Learn about them ahead of time and engage and motivate them to work with you. This will also be critical at some point in your future when you either need a major schedule improvement or payment terms consideration from them as your business grows.

At the end of the day, business is still a people game from employees to customers to suppliers. How well you engage and motivate them can well be the prime determination for your success, both short- and long-term.

"Your Employees Will Treat Your Customers The Way They Themselves Are Treated."

Recently, I had the opportunity to fly with an airline that had once been my very favorite, but because of my different itineraries and their routes, I hadn't flown them in more than a year. I was taken aback by nearly surly service at the gate, apathetic flight attendants and an overall feeling of "who cares?" I then realized that the airline in question had had a series of cutbacks as part of a proposed merger and what I was seeing was probably a reflection of the way these employees were feeling about how they felt they were being treated by their company.

Did you ever stop and think about that? That how you treat your people (and/or how they feel they are being treated) can be reflected in how they interact with your customers.

Think about places where you shop, retailers known for their unbelievable customer service – maybe it's a local store, or maybe it's a national chain like Lowe's or an online store like Zappo's. All of them will have one thing in common. Their employees provided you with an unforgettable experience, usually with a smile. They were happy while doing their job. My guess is if you asked them, they would tell you that it was one of the best places they ever worked. They reflect how they are treated.

Building a Successful Organization

And how about bad experiences? I would bet you that in a majority of them, it wasn't the first time with that merchant and, if it was a national retailer, perhaps, they are operating under the cloud of potential bankruptcy. Their employees are probably feeling the angst of potentially losing their job, to say nothing of possibly being asked to work more hours with less support.

Now, I'm not suggesting that you and your employees all have to hold hands and sing Kumbaya around the campfire, but that you understand that all employees want to be valued and respected. That doesn't mean no reprimands when they fall short of 100% effort or violate a company rule or policy. But it does mean providing them the training and the tools to do their job, showing them appreciation for their daily effort and recognizing when they go "above and beyond."

In a small business, where resources are limited and employees, often, have to wear multiple hats and compensation is, just as often, less than market, this can be a real challenge. But so long as they feel valued and respected, both as people and employees, what will be imparted to your customers will be a sense of pride and service.

Keep them posted on the company's progress with frequent company-wide meetings (even there are only five of you) and make sure that communication lines are wide open inside the company. Help them understand the importance of their role in the company's success. Listen to their ideas and encourage them to find new ways to improve processes for their particular function and for the company.

In essence, you want to operate under the premise that says "we treat our employees the way we want our customers treated," because it will surely translate...directly!

Building a Successful Organization

"Do You Allow Your Employees to Fail?"

Once, long ago, I was being interviewed for a position to run a division of one of the few large companies I ever worked for. As the interview was coming to a close, the Chairman/CEO, who I had known for years, asked me if I had any other questions. I said I just had one. "Do you allow your employees to fail?"

He looked at me like I had two heads and said, "Excuse, me, I'm not sure I understand your question." I explained that what I meant was if an employee made a bad decision (big or small), was he/she severely reprimanded, or worse, fired? I explained that if that was the case, he should simply fire me, right then, because I was sure to make a bunch of bad decisions. I further noted that in the position that I was taking on, I would be making, potentially, hundreds of decisions every week, but that I would, invariably, make some of those wrong. But, I was not afraid to either make them, or to be held accountable for them. But I was not "mistake-proof." Nor are any of your employees.

Often, without being aware of it, small business owners create an environment where they inhibit or almost prohibit employee decision-making and blame is more important than ultimate success. How?

By not encouraging or allowing employees to make decisions (you make them instead); by berating (often publicly) mistakes, and worst of all, firing employees who make a serious mistake, maybe even one that costs the company money. This last one is especially troubling because it is, typically, made in anger, and it fosters a "blame game" mentality in the company.

Think about it. If you had decisions regarding your area of responsibility, constantly being made by the owner, or you saw a peer get dressed down, or worse, fired for a mistake, how often do you think you would take a chance and make a decision on your own. And, allowing employees to fail is way different than encouraging them to fail. You want them to make good decisions and you want them to take some risks. And you want them to learn from their mistakes. More important you want them to take responsibility for their job and their decisions. How do you this?

By holding them accountable. And how do you hold them accountable? You give them the authority to make decisions related to their job responsibility. And you make sure that when they do make a bad decision or a mistake, it is dealt with as a way to learn and grow. The most important lesson delivered should be – learn, grow, don't make this one again...most important, move on. Even, if the mistake costs the company money.

Allowing employees to fail means encouraging employees to make decisions, holding them accountable, but understanding that we are all human and will make mistakes. As they learn from their mistakes, they become more confident and stronger in their decision-making, and the company benefits from having employees who are both accountable and growing, every day. And you, as the small business owner, have people you can count on.

Chapter 8 – Finance – It's Way More Than "Bean Counting;" Way More Than Raising Capital

"To the Entrepreneur, Cash is Almost as Important as Breathing (But Only a Close Second)"

Cash flow, its generation, its conservation and, overall, its management is the single most important discipline an entrepreneur must learn to be truly successful. And of these, cash generation is the most important. From day one, it is the lifeblood of the business and will and should be at the forefront of, virtually, every decision an entrepreneur makes regarding it.

Now this seems obvious, doesn't it?

Yet, too many entrepreneurs have this notion that the very first thing that they need to do is to raise money. Nope! The first thing they need to do is generate cash, which, typically, means getting customers!

Unfortunately, most entrepreneurs, especially in the early going, spend more time and precious resources trying to raise cash from outside sources, usually prematurely, rather than trying to generate it from potential customers.

But you say, I need to raise cash so that I can execute my business plan and grow my business. True, but why not just have a total focus on generating cash any way you can to get the business off the ground and keep it running? That could include raising cash from outside investors, which ultimately will help the business to grow. But at the end of the day, developing and maintaining a "whatever it takes" cash generating focus will serve as the entrepreneur's foundation for future business success.

So, let's say you're just starting out. You have a little seed money from savings or investments, enough to carry you for several months. But you need to get your product concept into reality and get a customer to use (and, hopefully, pay for) it. But, you're short of the necessary resources it would take to complete the product.

You have three choices to generate the necessary cash. You can get a second job or consulting gig. You can try to raise money from friends and family (no angel or institutional investor touches you without proof of concept). Or, since hopefully, your product concept has been "bounced off of" several prospective customers, you can partner with one of those customers to provide development dollars in return for ongoing influence in future product enhancements and future product royalties, as an example.

Now there's not much difference in the ultimate probability or timing of success in any of the three. However, with the third, you not only have a product, but you have a customer and have generated cash from that customer. You have a reference (and since they have a vested interest) – a good one. And you are on your way to understanding what's most important about cash flow – cash generation – and a leg up for future capital raising from investors, since you now have proof of concept completed.

Finally, you'll notice I haven't mentioned either cash conservation or cash management, which I said were important parts of cash flow. Well, if you don't generate it, you won't have to worry much about either conserving it or managing it. More about those two in the next section. Go generate it first!

Finance – It's Way More Than "Bean Counting; Way More Than Raising Capital!

"To the Entrepreneur, Cash is Almost as Important as Breathing (But Only a Close Second)" - Part II

In a previous section, we made the point that cash flow, its generation, its conservation and, overall, its management is the single most important discipline an entrepreneur must learn to be truly successful. In that posting we dealt with cash generation. Today, we'll address an increasingly critical problem – cash management – controlling collections and payments.

It's one thing to cause a cash generation event (a sale), another entirely to collect on that event. In times like these, creativity is a necessity in getting paid. Providing incentives to customers (discounts for early payments) may not be enough to get them to move payments from a 30 or 45 day cycle to 15 days. However, if you're in the services business, you can attack the problem from a pricing and invoicing timing perspective.

All customers look for "deals." Give them one, but make it a positive for you. If you're providing a monthly service, instead of billing them monthly, after the fact, "cut a deal" for a six or twelve month pricing, with estimated services billed in advance (30 days or one quarter ahead), based on historical usage, with a 5-10% discount. Provide a reconciliation 30 days in arrears and adjust future bills accordingly (up or down). While it might reduce margins some, it gets precious cash in early and also provides an incentive for you to get efficiencies into your service offering. Plus, since you're billing in advance, the customer can't get very far behind without the potential of you shutting off the service.

If you deliver a product, establish a pricing policy that ensures that you don't ship the product without a majority, if not all of the product paid for prior to shipment. If it's a high value product ($25,000 +), establish staged pricing – with multiple payment points, deposit at contract signing, additional payment either time-based (30 days later) or event-based (goes into production) and remainder prior to shipment. If there is a "shakedown" or acceptance period for the product, you might have a reserve of 10% (no more) to be paid within x days after that period. In no event should you ship the product without, at least, all of your costs covered.

Not all customers will like these pricing models, but you'll never know unless you try it out with actual customers. If you can get even a portion of your customers on them, you have taken a big step to getting and keeping collections under control. And remember, no matter what you offer customers, it has to be a "win-win" for both of you for it to work.

As for payments, it's a much simpler deal. Like your customers, you are going to stretch payments as far as you can without either incurring service charges or negatively impacting your supplier relationship. However, always try to negotiate terms, whether it's 2% net 15 (2% discount if you pay within 15 days) or something a little more creative. Your

Finance – It's Way More Than "Bean Counting; Way More Than Raising Capital!

suppliers are also looking for cash. You just want to give them less than full invoice as late as possible.

Managing your cash starts with cash generation and ends with the ability to collect that cash as quickly and effectively as possible.

Secrets to Entrepreneurial Success

"Is The Financial System for Your Small Business Just a 'Virtual Cigar Box?'"

Back when Yoda was just a mere wisp of a lad, I remember a newsstand where I would go to buy a newspaper for my Dad. The proprietor, who was the father of one of my good friends, had a unique way of tracking his money. Under his counter he had an old cigar box and in it he kept all the newsstand's money for the day.

When folks made a purchase, he put the money he received in the box. When a supplier made a delivery, he took money out of the box to pay for the delivery. Each night he totaled what he had left, tracked it in a copy book like the ones we used in school. He transferred the majority to a little safe he kept and, eventually, deposited it into his bank. The rest stayed in the cigar box to make change and pay for any deliveries for the next day.

A pretty simple system for a pretty simple business. No employees. Low-priced/low cost products. He never tracked how much he made on newspapers, cigarettes, candy or gum. He didn't care as long as he was taking in more than he was paying out. Plus, in those days, there really wasn't any real cost-effective way for him to do that.

Finance – It's Way More Than "Bean Counting; Way More Than Raising Capital!

Today, many small business owners, with way more complicated business models, who have had the "cash is king" philosophy hammered at them, incessantly (including by yours truly), operate much the same way. As long as cash in is greater than or equal to cash out, things are good. And while, at the very basic level that is correct, the ability to track costs, and analyze revenues is critical to longer-term success. It's where a business most needs to grow up.

While most entrepreneurs understand the very basics of accounting (revenue, expense, profit), few have strong financial backgrounds. At the outset of their business, they pick up Quicken or QuickBooks, establish some high level "expense buckets," and never pay it a second thought, tracking what comes in and what goes out. And while each of these (and other basic accounting) software products are pretty powerful, in effect, they operate the same way as my neighborhood newsstand, except their cigar box is virtual! They really have no idea what it really costs to acquire a customer or deliver and support a product. Worse, they have no basic data to know whether a particular product or service is priced properly and is making a profit. And worse yet, if they ever have even the faintest notion of raising outside capital or even applying for a loan, forget it! Not with those financial records!

If this sounds like you and you've been in business for more than a couple of years and/or have revenues of more than $500 thousand a year, it's time your business grew up, financially.

Here are some critical recommendations to help you do that:

Hire a Bookkeeper

It's time for you to let go. Even a part-timer can help you get your financial records into a more orderly and professional context and set up more detailed revenue and expense categories to help you understand and track your finances. This will help you to not only know THAT you are making money, but WHERE and WHY.

Create a Rudimentary Cost System

Track labor hours by customer, product, project, whatever the key metrics are for your business, from you right down to the person who answers the phone. Attempt to assign supplier costs the same way.

Review Pricing

With better financials and better tracking of costs, see if pricing really reflects those costs as opposed to "thinking" that they do. A price increase for a poorly priced product helps you win twice. Higher revenue per product/service, plus higher margins.

Begin Forecasting

To help you better manage costs and growth, and based on your new historical financial recordkeeping, begin to forecast where you expect your business to be over some future time horizon. Relative to revenue, expense, profit and cash flow, start with months, work into quarters and then into years. This way you can begin to do more effective cash flow planning for seasonal disparities in revenue.

Managing and growing a business is more than "cash in" being greater than "cash out." It requires you to really know where that cash is coming from and where it's going...in depth. Get rid of that "virtual cigar box," and get your

Finance – It's Way More Than "Bean Counting; Way More Than Raising Capital!

financials working at the same level you are. Time for the business to grow up, financially!

"Numbers Are Important. Which Ones Do You Use to Manage Your Small Business?"

I hear it all the time from entrepreneurs. "I'm not really a numbers person." Especially, the long-time ones. They go on to tell me about how they use "their gut" to drive most critical decisions. Yet, when I ask more penetrating questions, I come to find that there are always a couple of key numbers that they track, religiously.

They do this because they've learned that if these critical numbers or "key metrics," are where they are supposed to be, that the business is sailing right along. If not, they know what they need to fix to get it back on the right track. And the interesting part about this (and which should come as no surprise) is that the type of numbers that are, typically, tracked does vary by type of business.

For example, tracking cost of goods sold (COGS) is almost meaningless in a software business, but is one of the most critical metrics in manufacturing. Shipping costs are simply part of doing business (and usually passed along to customers) in most product businesses. Yet, in a distribution business, they are, often, the difference between a profitable and an unprofitable business.

Finance – It's Way More Than "Bean Counting; Way More Than Raising Capital!

For me, no matter the type of business, I always tracked three numbers on a weekly or monthly (depending on how close to the edge the business was running) basis. Those were net forecasted cash flow (the difference between forecasted cash in and cash out); forecasted to close in the next 30 days (my most critical sales situations) and backlog (what we were contracted to ship/bill over the next 30-60 days). Now I looked at lots of numbers (I am a numbers person) during a week or a month, but only was focused on these three.

No matter your type of small business, you need to be a "numbers person." But there is also an extreme. Many entrepreneurs and small business owners needlessly complicate the process with a "dashboard" of fifteen or twenty critical metrics that they track to manage their business. That's like trying to manage and achieve fifteen or twenty objectives. Plus, you have to wonder how many of those are redundant (a part of a higher level, more critical metric) or not really critical? Keep it simple!

Determine the key elements that drive your business. Determine and track the numbers that support those. Maximum of three to five, on a weekly or monthly basis. That's all you need!

"Are You Using the Lack of Capital As An Excuse?"

The lack of capital hurts, virtually, every small business at one time or another. Some, though, use this lack of capital as justification for why their business is not doing as well as it should.

These have, indeed, been trying economic times. Maybe the worst Yoda has seen since he has been in business with, no capital to be found from almost any source, over a lengthy period of time (regardless of how much your local banker protests that they're lending – a couple of credit line increases a year to their best business customers doesn't constitute lending). And, while it spawned some real challenges, it has also provided a "crutch" to some entrepreneurs who believe that they can make all their problems go away with if they can just throw capital at them. It's sort of a takeoff on the old "you can't be too thin enough or too rich" (but that's for another blog time), which as we all know is simply a justification for excess...either way.

Small business owners who exhibit this classic symptom may be using it as an excuse for not really knowing what it will take to succeed and figuring that capital is the solution to getting more sales, becoming more profitable, serving customers better. And I'm here to tell you that if the basics aren't in place to do each of these, all more capital will do is provide the same result, more expensively, or worse, provide a little better set of results and hide the real problems.

While pretty much all businesses can benefit from having more capital, the truest measure of a successful business is not just bottom line (or top line), but how well the business manages both when the economy is "in the tank." In fact, lean times often help a business get back to basics. Good times often make companies, like people, get "fat, dumb and happy," drifting into bad spending habits, shortcutting critical processes...just getting sloppy.

So, use the lack of capital or "belt tightening" times as a crusade, of sorts, to do more with less, to become leaner, meaner and hungrier. Use it as an excuse to review every step and person involved in the key processes of the business – those that generate sales and deliver and support products, from how you get prospects, to how you interact with customers, to how you take care of tools on the shop floor or maintain workstations in your development group.

In short, you're looking to eliminate redundancies (not necessarily people) and wring as much "fat" (that you might have developed in the good times) out of the system. And make it a company-wide exercise, challenging everyone to make their job more efficient and their roles more effective. That's way better than them having the proverbial "sword of Damocles" hanging over their head as the business slows to a crawl and they worry about their jobs.

What you'll end up with is an operation that understands what it takes to succeed, no matter the economic or capital environment. And a stronger team to make that happen, because you involved the whole company. And...no excuses!

Finance – It's Way More Than "Bean Counting; Way More Than Raising Capital!

"6 Key Things Entrepreneurs Should Consider Before Seeking Outside Investment."

There's probably no one area where more mistakes are made, more misconceptions exist or that troubles entrepreneurs and small business owners more than that of raising outside investment. Now, not every business needs to raise outside capital. But if you do, here are some key things to consider to keep you out of trouble, dispel faulty notions and make it go a little easier.

Understand, raising capital is no "day at the beach." But if you approach it with the right frame of mind, the right business model and the right expectations, your chances of success increase dramatically. But it is still a difficult mountain to climb, so here are six key considerations before you begin:

1. Investors Fund Businesses, Not Ideas.
I have seen more "business plans" than I can even count that were not plans at all, but ideas surrounded by hopes and dreams. A fundable business plan has, at a minimum, a business that has passed "proof of concept" (defined as cash paying customers successfully buying and using your product for a period of time) and has a scalable business model. That is, one that shows how, with proper sales and

marketing and/or some additional infrastructure (often, the basis for your funding requirements) you can make money.

2. Investors Invest in People Not Businesses.

No matter how good your business model, if the investor does not believe you and your team can pull it off, there will be no investment. An old saying – "they invest in the jockey, not the horse," still holds true. The more management experience (previous entrepreneurial or small company efforts) and industry (in your target market niche) credibility and experience you and your team bring, the higher your probability of success. If you've had experience with professional/institutional investors in the past, no matter your success, it heightens your odds, especially if you go back to them.

3. The Earlier the Investment, The Higher The Risk, The Higher Ownership Stake

Risk is highest in the early going. For anyone who comes in at this point, the odds of them losing most or all of their investment are very high (no matter how great you think your concept is). This is why, in the early going, you should bootstrap your operation the best you can. If you have some access to capital (your own, partners, etc.) manage it like you were never going to see another penny. But if you don't have much, you have to be creative. Wherever possible, get suppliers, developers, sales people, etc., to work on an incentive basis or for equity (see an earlier post – "100% of Zero, Is Still Zero" – for the rationale for this). Otherwise, you may give up a sizable stake in your company for a small amount capital and will still need more money to fund your early growth.

4. Don't Run Out of Money While You're Raising Money

This is the corollary to the previous consideration. If you've been in operation for a while, but are now running out of cash, this is exactly the wrong time to raise outside capital. Investors, especially professional ones, can smell "blood in the water" like sharks. They can read this situation readily. If they like your business model, they will delay until the very last minute (if they even consider it) and strike an onerous deal because you are desperate. Better to tap every personal resource you have and/or every friend, every family member for a short-term loan and get your ship righted before you embark on an outside raise.

5. Do You Need Capital or Do You Need Specific Resources?

Too many entrepreneurs miss this one. Typically, when you're raising capital, you're doing it to go out and "buy" resources – people, systems, equipment, etc. Why not eliminate "the middle man" – the capital raise and the associated time it will take (another story for another time)? Find a partner or partners who might have complementary market presence and those resources already in place. Often a relationship can be structured on a revenue share basis that becomes a win-win for both parties.

6. There's No Such Thing as a Silent Investor

Finally, make no mistake, whether it's kindly old Uncle Bert, an angel investor, who simply likes to get small businesses off the ground or a venture capitalist, they will all want to know what and how you are doing (with increasing frequency, depending on the overall financial markets). Depending on how "professional" (doing it for a living) an investor they are, they will be in your underwear! Many will require a board seat. No matter the promises of letting you run your business, they WILL be involved, even if it's a series of periodic phone call (that may be more or less inquisition-like). And with the first missed forecast, even if it's a monthly one, you can expect even more communication, physical presence and active involvement.

They want to be sure their money is being used and managed properly.

Raising outside investment is a difficult and time-consuming process. It is not for everyone. But without some basic understanding, it can not only be extremely frustrating but could end in angry failure. Consider these six key issues before setting out to raise outside capital and your chances of success should increase, dramatically.

Finance – It's Way More Than "Bean Counting; Way More Than Raising Capital!

"Is Your Business Plan Written for Your Prospective Investor…or More Likely, Your Prospective Customer?"

Most entrepreneurs spend countless hours putting their business plan together for outside capital, and much of it is wasted because it's, often targeted at the wrong audience. And what's worse, is that it's usually a "telling" document, not a "selling" document. This, most often, comes about from three common mistakes that many small business owners make:

- The entrepreneur is, usually, so close to the market and is pitching that market every day that they assume whoever they're in front of understands the jargon, terms and nuances of that market.

- The feeling that "more is better,", that an investor wants to know every feature and function for the product that underpins their business concept (often, what they do with prospective customers as well).

- The belief that their plan needs to have as much mind-numbing detail as possible. And, the more complex the financial model, the better!

Overall, the purpose of a capital raising business plan is…TO RAISE CAPITAL. Period. End of story. Sure, it should be the blueprint for the entrepreneur's strategies and tactics and the steps you take to implement them, but, typically, it's out of date before it comes out of the printer. No, that plan, which is a "living, breathing document" should be your small business "battle plan," the one you operate with, day-to-day (I've written multiple blog posts about the importance of this, previously – see those).

This plan, plain and simple, is to sell investors on why they should invest in you, the entrepreneur, your management team and your business.

So, what you're developing is a detailed "brochure" for your company. Something that makes folks "want to buy." Here are some basic considerations that you should be in any "selling" capital raising business plan:

- **What is the problem you're solving or the need you're addressing and the opportunity that that presents?**

Give some background on the market, overall size, etc., why the problem or need exists and, more specifically, size the addressable market for the opportunity. If you're going to use jargon, keep it to a minimum, define it, explain it and put it in context.

- **How will your solution solve the problem or address the need?**

Keep feature/function and specs to a minimum, or translate them to benefits and the solution. Wherever possible, translate benefits to cost savings, revenue generation for your addressable market. Quantifiable benefits make an impression. Who else is doing this? What inroads have they made? And if no one is else is doing this, why are you so smart? What have you found that everyone else has missed? This could be "your secret sauce!"

- **What are your key strategies to sell, deliver and support your solution?**

This is where the "rubber meets the road," where your credibility gets tested. And the most critical of these is how you will sell, to whom and why they will buy. Here you're tying together how your solution solves the problem or addresses the need and how you will drive that solution to the marketplace. And most importantly, how it will scale as you penetrate the market.

- **How will you make money?**

Then the investor knows how he/she will make money. Explain how you price, the rationale behind it and the margins that support it. Show how scalability translates to cost-efficiencies and greater margins. Sure, have spread sheets, forecasts, etc., but somewhere distill it down to what the basic business proposition is... in short, how you make money!

- **Who are you; who is your team and why are you so good?**

Especially highlight if you or your team has either market experience and/or credibility in your target market or has had experience starting, developing and growing previous small businesses. If you don't have any of this, go get it. Investors invest in the jockey, not the horse. You and your team are the jockey.

- **How much money do you need and how will you use it?**

Be specific. No "abouts" or ranges. You must show precision. After all, it's their money. Delineate where it will be spent by function or specific task(s) and why those areas are important. No more than 10% in working capital or other "catch all" categories. This is where your audience really learns how much you know about running your business.

- **How will you exit?**

Put real thought into this, not just the usual, "we plan on a strategic acquisition for exit." Think it through and justify who might acquire you and why, or how else your investors can monetize their investment.

Developing a "selling" capital raising plan starts with understanding who your market is – the investment community - and creating a "selling" document that makes them want to buy (invest)!

Chapter 9 – Operations - Where the Rubber Meets the Road

"Are You The Major Bottleneck in Your Own Company?"

Recently, I was contacted by a company that I had worked with early in their history that had grown very nicely and quite profitably. However, when they reached a certain revenue level and they seemed to "stall out," and had trouble not only growing further, but making money.

The small business owner, a really smart, driven fellow was totally frustrated by it and called me back in to help him figure it out. He complained that there seemed to be bottlenecks and problems that he couldn't uncover.

Everything seemed to take longer and cost more to do than it had previously. They were getting bigger jobs, but making much less profit on them. The company was experiencing high turnover and despite a very well-thought out quality program, their quality was suffering.

Now what I remembered about this owner from my previous engagement was how impressed I was with his attention to detail and his understanding of, virtually, every process in his company. This had helped the company to grow, not only profitably, but with a very loyal customer base. He was involved in every aspect of the company. But, as it turns out, what got him to success, it what was driving him to failure.

Operations – Where the Rubber Meets the Road

As the company grew, his obsession with detail continued. He was involved in, virtually, every decision that the company made, from the important ones like capital equipment for the production floor, but also, to the seemingly unimportant ones (for an owner) like what color the new break room would be painted. And this slowed down every decision, often causing the company to miss key deadlines. Plus, although he hired a number of good managers, many had left in frustration with the decision-process slowed down by his insisting to be involved or, worse, countermanding their decisions. In addition, those who remained simply pushed decision-making back up to the owner, slowing things down further.

Since, initially, he created most of the tasks involved in getting his product out the door, when the company was in its infancy, he, probably, felt he knew how to do those tasks better than anyone in the company. While he now had a nice sized staff, he would still, periodically, get involved in helping to get product out the door. Often, changing process, on the fly, back to the way the company used to do things, causing significant discord and furthering turnover in managers.

He had become his own major bottleneck!

Like that famous quote from the old comic strip, Pogo – "we have seen the enemy and he is us." Often what gets you there, doesn't keep you there. Sometimes the company outgrows the owner.

And this is extremely hard for folks who remember the early days, often going without salary, working long hours and weekends, living and dying on every order. They still want to be involved in every decision, every customer situation, every personnel decision. But they can't. Not if they want the company to grow.

Entrepreneurs who want to truly grow their company need to constantly evolve and grow themselves. If they remain the same, so will the company. They have to look for new solutions, new managers and new ways of doing business.

Operations – Where the Rubber Meets the Road

"To Increase Success, Entrepreneurs Should Use Industry Best Practices as Processes to Improve On!"

I love when I read or hear about advice given to entrepreneurs about industry best practices. First of all, best practices for a small business are those things that work for them, as I noted in a previous blog post awhile back. Second, most of these so-called "best practices," typically come from major corporations (usually developed by Booz-Allen-like consulting firms) as the best way to get things done through their labyrinths of bureaucracy and mind-numbing process. Not exactly role models for agile, fast-moving, often resource-constrained entrepreneurial operations.

So when your small business is presented with some potential best practice, study it, embrace it, if in some way it makes sense for you, but most of all, improve on it by modifying it to fit your business. Don't just try to implement it because some industry guru tells you it's the "latest and greatest!" Because at the end of the day, best practices are relative.

No two entrepreneurial companies operate the same way. What is my best practice may be your administrative nightmare. What is your best practice may choke my "just in time" operation.

Look at "best practices" as models. See how the model fits within your specific business model. Then improve on it!

Operations – Where the Rubber Meets the Road

"R-E-S-P-E-C-T– Don't Forget Your Vendor Is A Business Owner Too! Make The Vendor A Partner Instead of Just A Supplier."

I had a small business client whose relationship with a key vendor was, at best, rocky. The client was one of the vendor's largest and most visible customers. Yet, response time to specific requirements, problems or issues, while never all that good seemed to actually be getting worse. It seemed somehow counterintuitive that the vendor would be reacting this way, so I set up a time to meet with him without the client.

What I found was a situation that probably exists for many entrepreneurs in some of their key vendor relationships. The vendor, who had known the owner for many years, just simply got tired of never being able to do enough to please the customer. No matter what hoops he jumped through, unrealistic delivery deadlines made or how many times he "went the extra mile," he simply could never gain his customer's satisfaction. Worse, it appeared that while the customer, whose business was thriving, in part because of the products and services provided by the vendor, begrudged anything "extra" he had to pay for services rendered over and above the standard products and services. So, the vendor, feeling hugely disrespected, just kind of gave up. "He just doesn't understand that I'm running a business too. That I have payroll and rent payments to meet and that I'm allowed to make a profit as well."

And this vendor is not alone. Many entrepreneurs, so laser-focused on their own business success, fail to realize the fundamental importance of developing a partnership with their key suppliers, especially those who are small businesses as well. Here lies a significant opportunity for businesses to help each other succeed by forging a relationship built on trust and respect for what each is doing and bringing to the party for the other's success. I've talked a great deal in these posts about customer service, that is, vendor to customer. But there's another viewpoint. Vendor respect; that is, treating your supplier as a peer entrepreneur, understanding that they have other customers besides you. And like you, have goals and aspirations and need to grow their business and make a profit to do so.

Taking all this into consideration, if you have a key supplier, who provides you a product or service that is fundamental to the operation of your business or the delivery of your products or services, they are more than simply a supplier. They are a critical part of your business. Think about treating them like a peer, like a partner. Respect their business and they will respect yours.

Help them understand how important their product or service is to your business. If you don't know, learn where you fit in their customer scheme (largest, smallest, somewhere in between) and how many other customers he/she is serving. Show them what happens when one of their deliveries is late. Have them explain the fundamentals of how they deliver their product and any role your company might play in impacting delivery schedules (like

Operations – Where the Rubber Meets the Road

constantly wanting to change features or expedite product schedule). Show them how you drive revenue and the impact of what happens when their product malfunctions. Have them explain what's critical to their own revenue generation and how certain demands impact that. And above all, thank them for supporting you.

At the end of the day, you're both striving for the same thing. You both need each other. The beginning lyrics to the old Aretha Franklin song fit perfectly. R-E-S-P-E-C-T.

Respect your vendor's need to make a profit on what he/she delivers to you, either as a basic product or service, or a highly customized one. You'll be surprised how much the relationship will change and how much their response time to specific requirements, problems or issues improves and how much more proactive they become with you and your business.

"'Win, Win' Should be an Objective in Every Business Relationship!"

As with most of my blog posts, a recent encounter with a client and one of their key suppliers triggered this one. The supplier had negotiated a "sweetheart deal," hammering out an almost-untenable agreement with my client, who needed the critical service that the supplier provided.

Further, at every turn, the supplier was determined to drive the relationship and ensure that they "won" every point from proving that it was the fault of the client's drawings that caused the supplier's quality problem (a real stretch) to marking up and getting every last dollar from the client, a fledgling company operating on relatively thin financing.

The upshot?

With additional financing, we found a better solution by moving the service in house and rendered the supplier relationship an afterthought. Key to this supplier (also an entrepreneur himself) was that he "grew up" in a huge corporation.

It is often said that we are the product of our environment; that what we are often the sum total of our experience. Nowhere is that more true than with entrepreneurs.

Operations – Where the Rubber Meets the Road

Many entrepreneurs, like our supplier example, grew up in a big company culture, learning real-world business skills, often, from, politically-charged situations, driven by folks with personal and professional agendas. In most of these environments, the object is to win (whether or not that "win" benefits the company) and the opponent (often in a corporate turf war) loses. In effect, a "zero sum game," which is the way our supplier operated.

In this environment, the concept of "win, win" is, virtually, unheard of. Yet, the key to entrepreneurial success, and maybe even life success, is "win, win" in all relationships. And it is here that the fledgling entrepreneur, often, has to unlearn bad habits and learn new ones.

For some folks, "win, win" is some Pollyanna-ish notion that can't exist in the "dog-eat-dog" business world. And they could not be more wrong. Having negotiated hundreds of deals from the complex – acquisitions, capital investment, joint ventures, outsourcing - to the straightforward – contractor, distributor, employment relationships, the common point of all success is that both parties have to walk away feeling that they had "won." Maybe not all they could, but enough so that the other guy could feel the same way.

But for many entrepreneurs, this type of thinking is foreign from the way they were "brought up" in the big company mindset. So, for you folks, and as a refresher for you others who already believe in and practice "win, win," here are some key ways to ensure all your negotiations and relationships end up that way.

Know What Your Objectives Are
Going in, know what's absolutely essential, what's important and what's just "nice to have." Then you know

what points you have to hold firm on, what points can be negotiated and what ones don't really matter.

Put Yourself in the Other Person's Position
This is where "win, win" begins. Try to understand what their objectives are, what they need to get out of the negotiation or relationship. Try to put their objectives in the same three categories as yours above. Hopefully, you can both achieve what is essential.

Give a Little, Take a Little
Negotiations and relationships are built on this concept. There are always "tradeoffs." Let the other party feel like they have "won" some of their points. If they walk away from the table with a deal, where they felt like all they did was "give," it will come back and haunt you later, trust me.

Keep the Relationship Open, Honest and Respectful
Incredibly important. To keep relationships going requires that when screw-ups occur, as they will always, that there is honest accountability and "give and take," to ensure that steps are taken to not have them repeated. No blame game, just honest admission and the spirit of "moving forward."

"Win, win" is not a one-time thing. It is a business lifestyle. Learn it and live it and your success will follow.

Operations – Where the Rubber Meets the Road

"Are You Allowing Employees, Suppliers or Customers to Hold You Hostage?"

Relationships evolve, be they personal or business. As they do, we often miss key signs that they are headed to an unhealthy place because we aren't paying attention or seriously need or want the relationship to continue. And suddenly we find ourselves "hostage" to the relationship. Nobody likes to operate out of fear or feel that someone has a serious hold on them. In personal relationships this often makes the relationships unhealthy and destructive. We, usually, avoid these situations at all costs. Yet, entrepreneurs and small business owners often find themselves in these kinds of situations, be it with employees, suppliers or customers.

They allow threats of cutting off the relationship, either direct or implied, to force them to make decisions or operate in a particular way. No matter how important a person or organization is to your business, you should never allow fear to drive decision-making.

This often happens with key employees, who, either through their own personal insecurity or a mistrust of the company and/or its management, feel they need to protect themselves and become keepers of information and processes difficult to replicate. In my turnaround experience there was always the guy I call "Fred." Fred was the person who, during employee interviews and data gathering, people would say, whatever happens, "we can't lose Fred, he's the only one who knows 'X'." Guess who was the first one off the boat if cuts were necessary? You can't have a situation where one employee has that kind of power. It permeates the entire organization. Everybody knows it and it eventually hurts morale and attitude.

NDAs and non-competes are deterrents, but don't solve the problem. Documenting job functions and tasks, and cross training help. But, creating a culture of mutual respect and trust goes a long way to not having these kinds of problems. And the essence of this kind of culture is communication.

Suppliers and large customers are a whole other thing.

With suppliers, it's, typically, a relationship that started innocuously when the company was just beginning and either the entrepreneur knew the supplier from past history or the supplier provided some advantage to the new business, be it unique capability, price, flexibility to work with a small company or simply geographic convenience. The relationship evolves and one day, the small business owner wakes up to huge price increase or delivery changes from the only supplier for a key part or process. They have no alternative because they never thought to get one.

Never have just one supplier for any key part, process or assembly. Always have at least two vendors for anything critical to product delivery or price. This keeps the relationships healthy, with them knowing if they can't meet delivery date or price, somebody else will.

Operations – Where the Rubber Meets the Road

Finally, having a single large customer is a "two-edged sword," that cuts both ways. It provides the small business with significant, often, nearly-guaranteed annual revenue. Typically, because the customer is so key, the small business "bends over backwards" to ensure customer satisfaction through the highest level quality and customer service. Further, though, the entrepreneurial operation can also get a little lazy and not press hard enough to expand its customer base. Hey, life is good when revenue comes in like clockwork!

But, at the same time, the customer can also attempt to extract more and more price concessions from the entrepreneur either using a subtle or not-so subtle threat of either reducing the amount of revenue provided by the relationship or opening the situation up for new bidding on the contract. And then the small business finds itself in a very tight box.

The lesson here is obvious. Small companies cannot be too dependent on one or two major customers. And that's often a painful, but necessary lesson to learn. If you see that evolving, put a plan in place that's almost a "disaster recovery" one. The plan's foundation should be – "what if Customer X went away?" You need to implement that plan immediately and operate as if the customer was going away tomorrow.

Being held hostage is never any fun. Know the symptoms of a potential bad relationship evolving with either employees, suppliers or customers and fix the problem before it reaches the unhealthy stage. Fear should never drive decision-making!

Chapter 10 – Starting the Business is the Easy Part; Growing It is Where the Greatest Challenges Are

Secrets to Entrepreneurial Success

"The Gerbil Syndrome"

Ever watch a gerbil turn their special wheel? They turn that wheel by running as fast as they can, yet the wheel is only going around and around, not forward. So many entrepreneurs find themselves in this position, especially after an initial growth spurt that took them to a certain sales level, only to stay stagnated at 5-10%, plus or minus from that sales level for multiple years.

Suddenly, they wake up one day and they're still working extremely hard, but like the gerbil, running as fast as they can, mostly in place. The most interesting thing is that nearly every entrepreneur has a plan when they start out. Few ever update that plan. They just keep doing what they've been doing. A new year starts, they just jump back on that old wheel and start turning.

Does this describe your business? If so, how do you stop being a gerbil and get your business moving forward instead of in place?

First and foremost, you have to want to change. You've got to be willing to shake things up a little bit. What got you to $2 million or $5 million or $10 million, or wherever you're stuck, won't get you to the next level.

To do this you need to objectively assess how you're doing business today, who's doing what and why, what's contributing to forward progress and what's not. This is

Growing the Business Is Where the Greatest Challenges Are

where you should discover the key things that are keeping you running in place. From this assessment you need to establish a new set of objectives and a solid plan to achieve them.

But, it's not easy to do this yourself...and keep it objective. After all, you put you on the wheel!

If you've got any advisors or a board, that might be a good place to ask for help with this assessment and planning activity to help keep the objectivity. If not, you can bring in an outside consultant to help lead you and your team through the planning process.

Get off the wheel. Get on the new plan!

"You Can't Be a 'One Ball Juggler' and Be a Successful Entrepreneur"

Jugglers have always fascinated me. Not the guys who can juggle three bowling balls or flaming torches, but those who can juggle five, six disparate things (usually relatively modest-sized) and keep them all in the air, without one falling to the ground. And how exciting would that same situation be if the juggler was doing it with one ball?

As a lifelong entrepreneur, I think my fascination was borne of identifying with a "kindred spirit." Because nowhere is keeping a number of objects 'in the air' more prevalent (or necessary) than in a small business. The further you move along the life cycle of a small business, the more balls you have to learn to juggle. And just like with the juggler, if all you can juggle is one ball (that is, one task at a time), it's not only not very exciting, but is a recipe for disaster with your business. Juggling multiple tasks is a skill you have to learn in order for your small business to succeed and it's something few are ever ready for.

As with jugglers, some folks come naturally at being able to do this, but for most of us, it is an acquired (and necessary)

Growing the Business Is Where the Greatest Challenges Are

habit. Unlike with jugglers, where there are actually people you can go to or classes you can attend to learn this skill, there really is no guidance for entrepreneurs.

So, for those of you, "multi-tasked challenged," let me offer some guidance. Here are *four critical indicators* that you might be a "one ball juggler" and the steps to take toward become an accomplished "small business juggler."

Can't Focus on More than One Thing at a Time

Everybody preaches focus to the entrepreneur, but it can be taken to an extreme. When you first start a business, it's obvious that there is much to be accomplished. But, typically, that can be done, serially, without the need for multi-tasking. Once you get rolling, you cannot succeed being focused on one thing at a time. There's just too much to be done. So you need to move out of your comfort zone and get at least a second ball in the air. Maybe it's not just concentrating on delivering this current project to your major customer, but also working on a marketing program to increase awareness for future prospects.

Can't Prioritize

Then, with a little success, it becomes a lot more complicated, with the entrepreneur being pulled in multiple directions by the needs of prospects, customers, vendors and employees. Plus, there's that dance recital that your daughter is in and that anniversary that's coming up. But not everything can be a number one priority. Nothing is more stressful or less productive than trying to make it all happen at once. Determine the top 3 (or 5 if you become really skillful at it) things that need to get done at any one time and let those be the tasks you juggle. The others simply get tabled until those get done. Then you add another as you complete one.

Can't Delegate/Don't Train Others

Once you have employees, even one, you need to learn to delegate some of the lesser tasks to them. Too many entrepreneurs, having had to do every single task, every single time, end up not able to break this habit. So when the priority tasks that need to be done multiply, the small business owner is overwhelmed, trying to do everything alone. Even if you believe that the only way for something to get done right is to do it yourself, once you have employees, you need to train them to take on some of your responsibility.

Don't Have "Business Peripheral Vision"

Ever watch a juggler's eyes? They're looking at the objects in the air, using their peripheral vision. You have to do the same thing with your business. You have to be aware of all the things going on around you that might affect key priority tasks, both those you are trying to accomplish and those you have delegated. For example, getting that proposal done and out, on time, will also require that you understand what peripheral tasks might impact that, like the logistics for printing, binding and making sure you make the FedEx deadline. Or, that your son's little league championship game is the day before and may require further schedule juggling to address both priorities. "Business peripheral vision" helps you keep all your tasks both, in perspective, as well as to understand which one or ones are the most complicated and bear extra concentration.

Don't be a "one ball juggler." It takes some careful awareness of the critical indicators and the ability to overcome them to "keep all the balls in the air," to succeed.

"In a Small Business, There Are No Absolutes. Everything is Relative. What Works, is What Works for You!"

While a trite expression, "no two businesses are alike," is a fundamental one. "Experts" are constantly telling you, the small business owner that you MUST do this, or you MUST do that, or you will fail. I have never believed that and my more than 30 years' experience as a small business CEO and advisor and my interaction with, literally, thousands of companies, has more than reinforced that. There is no one size fits all solution!

I have seen businesses succeed without a smattering of a plan (something I strongly urge all companies to have), others with detailed plan, updated monthly; with all employees as shareholders (another strong feeling of mine), or with none but the owner as a shareholder; without a single dollar of outside capital (no debt, no equity, just operating out of cash flow), or dozens of small equity participants, or millions of dollars in investment. I have watched other businesses find success with only "word of mouth" marketing, some with no sales force but the owner. What works is what works for you!

Now some of you, who pay attention to both my blog posts and my tweets know that I am also a strong believer in change, as a catalyst for growth. Now, how do I (and you) reconcile this point?

Well, back to what works. If it's working, my advice is keep doing it. But, of course, if your results start to suffer (as many small businesses have found, especially, over the past several years) then you almost have to look for new ways to do old things. Find new ways to do what works for you.

But even when you go down that path, you need to be careful how you sift through the plethora of advice that's out there, not just from Yoda, but other much smarter and more eloquent folks (you'll note I didn't say more experienced) than me.

Here's some guidance to help you.

- Approach the advice landscape as a Chinese menu. Seek advice according to what issues or problems you face, or what opportunities you're trying to capitalize on.

- Understand where the "advisor" is coming from. Most every professional advisor has specialized focus – sales, marketing, HR, etc. (although my perspective is always as a CEO or owner so that's a little different). Understand that when they're giving advice in their area of expertise and when they're venturing beyond (smart people tend to think if they're smart over here, then they must be smart over there as well).

- Pick those "nuggets" that seem to fit for you, your style and your small business. Don't allow the hot "strategy du jour" to drive change, simply for change's sake.

Growing the Business Is Where the Greatest Challenges Are

But no matter, at the end of the day, get as many perspectives as you can and find the one that works best for how you do business.

"Little Failures Are Often More Important to Entrepreneurs Than Big Successes. You Learn More!"

In my years of coaching baseball, I used to, sometimes, upset my players by telling them that I wished we lost more because we would learn more. Teams rarely analyze a victory in the same depth that they analyze a loss. We lost because we didn't do this, or because we did that too much, etc. We won because we were good. You get it.

Small businesses are much the same way. Big successes are celebrated, but rarely analyzed as to what made them a success. You beat the competition. Your product dazzled the IT manager or your presentation just knocked the board out of their seats! Again you get the picture.

But how about when your small business loses one? Or when a customer decides they no longer want to do business with you? How much do you learn from these little failures? Because it is here that real learning and true growth actually happens for entrepreneurs.

How often do you do a "post mortem" on a lost sale? I used to urge my sales people, after a loss, to ask the prospect if they would spend 15 minutes, maximum, on the phone to help them understand what we could have done better to have won their business. We would get three things out of this.

Growing the Business Is Where the Greatest Challenges Are

First, we would learn if there was something we could have done differently, even if it was just a price concession that might have changed the result. Second, we would learn if we had done something wrong – like maybe, we were too "heavy-handed" in our discussion of competition, or applied too much pressure to individual members of the committee making the decision. And third, but most important, we got in a final "touch point" with the prospect, that would show and solidify our professionalism (no hard feelings) and enable us to "keep the lines of communication open" for future business.

You can and should do this whenever and wherever failures, be they minor or major, occur. A project deadline missed by a mile. A particular new product feature that caused a product recall. A new hire that turned out badly, quickly.

Entrepreneurs need to learn from their failures:

- Why the failure occurred and what you can do to turn past failure into future success.

- No blame game, no matter what happened.

- When the successes come, small businesses should celebrate as a company. So to when the failures come, small business should learn from that as a company.

And those successes? Of course, you can learn from those as well. For they, potentially, create a model for future success.

But, at the end of the day, small business owners learn more from their failures. With success, ego always plays a role (hey, we're good). With failures, big and small, you feel way more vulnerable (we screwed up) and much more open to learn.

Growing the Business Is Where the Greatest Challenges Are

"Change Can Protect You From Small Business Failure!"

You hear so much, especially in these trying economic times, about business failure. Small companies that have been in operation for years and years, suddenly finding themselves having to close their doors. But how can that be?

They had passed through the "magical" first "n" years (you know all the quotes from this crowd and that about "x%" of all business fail during the first "n" years of their existence) and come through it successfully, maybe even making a little money. Growing their business, adding new employees. Isn't that supposed to ensure success? Nope!

Markets change; sometimes brought about by technology, sometimes by socio-economic changes, sometimes by new competition and, sometimes by subtle, things like mobility. And these changes, however external to the business, affect, not only the way business operates, but its ultimate success…or not.

And, just as often, businesses don't change. They keep doing the same thing, month in, month out, year in, year out, never thinking about doing anything differently. "If ain't broke, don't fix it!"

Not enough small businesses pay sufficient attention to the changes around them. They get comfortable. "Hey, we've been doing this like this for ten years and it's worked. No need to change." And then one day, their largest customer moves their business overseas and suddenly 25% of their business evaporates...overnight. They weren't paying attention to what was going on in their marketplace. How overseas competitors were making inroads. Or, perhaps, they saw it, but discounted it. "Hey, Jack's been a customer since we started in business. A few dollars difference in price isn't as important as the loyalty and customer service we've provided." Wrong! In tough economic times, loyalty and customer service, often, get replaced by "lowest price."

Now, some of you are saying, "but things like that you should see coming and react."

While that is true, many companies just don't. And it's not just about being constantly vigilant regarding what is going on in your market but as much about what is going on inside your own company.

For continued success, companies need to, periodically, re-invent themselves, or at least, periodically, take a hard look at what they're doing to make sure they understand what is working and what is not (or has stopped) working. But, unfortunately, it's the rare company that does that. Self-analysis is tough. Driving change is tougher yet. But a fundamental cornerstone of small business success is agility, which you've heard me espouse time and again. And this is where, for those of you who can master it, real dividends can be reaped. Keep your company fresh!

Look external...
You need to be market aware. Know what is going on in the markets you serve. Changes, subtle or otherwise, that appear

to be driving them – new technology, new competitors, new customer demands, whatever. Pay attention, talk to suppliers, talk to customers, talk to industry experts. Understand where your company and products now fit and might fit in the future. And start to anticipate how you need to change. Sometimes you need to re-invent the company to meet that change.

Look internal...
Look at processes that haven't changed in years. See where they can be streamlined or automated. Use technology to your advantage. Especially look at people who have been doing the same thing for an extended period of time. Have they retired in their job, but you're still paying them? When process or people behave in the "way we've always done it" mode, it's time for change. And sometimes, you just need to change it up, to re-invigorate your company.

Change is the recipe for continued small businesses success. Anticipate it, welcome it, drive it. It will keep your business fresh, alive ... and successful!

"You Know, You Are Allowed to Have Fun in Business!"

Reading a recent article in Sports Illustrated about football coach John Gagliardi, who coaches little Division III St. John's College in Minnesota, and who also happens to be the winningest football coach in NCAA history, I was taken by a phrase, "...his teams have more fun than any team in the country." Interesting. Now, you could say, of course they have fun. They always win. But that isn't it. They win BECAUSE they have fun.

We often use the same terms in business that are used on the sports field when we describe what is necessary to succeed. Intensity. Passion. The will-to-win. Yet, what may be missing is a critical emotion. Fun!

Business can be very serious stuff. Often an entrepreneur has much at risk, personally; may feel the responsibility for the livelihoods of employees, and have deep concern that the customers are being served effectively. But, at the end of the day, if it isn't fun, for the small business owner, the employees, and yes, even the customers, the chances of success are limited.

In sports, coaches have a choice as to the way they approach practices, dealing with the players and managing the game. And players respond, in kind. Coach Gagliardi simply made it fun to play. And their response was winning.

Growing the Business Is Where the Greatest Challenges Are

In small business, owners also have a choice as to the way the manage their business, deal with their employees and customers. A great example of a small business (now quite a large business) that had fun, right "out of the chute," is Southwest Airlines. Founder Herb Kelleher was never afraid to step out of character as CEO and both make fun of himself and keep a light hand, when it came to employees and customers. And if you watch their commercials, that sense of fun continues today. That doesn't mean that that either St. John's or Southwest didn't/doesn't take things seriously. It's just that they keep it in perspective and find ways to make it fun. In short, they succeed because they have fun, not the other way around.

Do you have fun in your organization? While there may be "no crying in baseball," there can be laughter in business! As the leader of your company, you set the pace for that. This doesn't mean you have to be a "standup comic," but you can make it both enjoyable and fun to come to work for your employees, and enjoyable and fun for your customers to do business with you.

For example, every company I ever ran (even most I advise today) used what I called "sales-grams." This was a light-hearted way to celebrate major sales. Someone (a different person every quarter) was responsible for "spreading the news," both locally and to any employees who were remote. Locally, the person responsible would have to find a novel way to "broadcast" sales' wins in the office. The louder, the better. We had everything from gongs to foghorns to my personal favorite, a real siren! Not only did it enable everyone to know we just closed a big sale, but it, invariably, caused everyone who heard to break out into laughter, because it was funny! Fun in business!

There are a myriad number of ways you can make your business more fun.

Most of them have at their foundation, a better sense of team and cooperation and reduction or the banishment of b.s. in daily operations. Beyond that, contests (not just $ incentive ones, but things like a "product naming," as an example) or company events that place all employees on equal footing (like a night out at the ballpark) are just a couple of ways to get and keep the fun in the business.

No matter what you do or how you do it, fun is underrated, and not often considered as part of the culture you build. Think again. A smile, a laugh, a light touch can make long hours driving toward a deadline or tough contract negotiations with a customer, worth it. Make fun a fundamental part of how you run your business.

"To Achieve Entrepreneurial Success, You Can Never Know Too Much!"

Knowledge is at the foundation of real entrepreneurial success. The popular old saying, "you can never be too rich or too thin" has a corollary in small business – "you can never know too much!" Further backed up by that old saw, "knowledge is power!"

That is, you can never have too much knowledge about your market, your competition and your current and prospective customers. Having it provides the power to move your enterprise from the ordinary to the extraordinary.

To me, that seems self-evident. Yet, many entrepreneurs either downplay it or flat out overlook it. Knowledge, data, information, call it what you will, should be at the foundation of everything you do in your business. The more you know, the better off you are.

In the old days when Master Yoda was but a young business warrior, you would have to spend days in the library poring over reference books or scanning microfiche of news articles to get market information. Today, the same and more information is available at your fingertips, a couple of Google searches away. There is almost no information, no data that you can't find. Yet few companies really put a high value or devote enough time or resources to gathering and developing the knowledge base that could make a huge difference for them in helping them grow and prosper.

Market and competitive knowledge helps you make better decisions about what products and services to develop, how to price and package them. Not just "gut feelings" or "me too" rationalizations. A product should never see the "light of day," without this kind of information as a background and basis for direction.

This means gathering as much data as possible about the problem and associated market your product or service addresses. How big is the market/problem today? How is it being addressed and how well by competitors or other related products or services? Visit competitors' websites. See how they package and position (and price) their products. Scour their social media. Learn how they think, so you understand how they might be selling. Visit relevant trade associations' sites. Understand what issues they believe are driving the market. Plan your product and marketing strategy accordingly.

Customer and prospect knowledge helps you better understand their business, their specific requirements BEFORE you ever walk in the door. Go to their website. Look at their social media, if they have any. Learn their "personality" (every company has one). Understand their organization, their key executives, helping you determine a little bit about their organizational dynamics and who the key "movers and shakers" might be within it. This will help you better prepare and target your sales campaigns; calling on the right people, framing better questions to gather even more knowledge when you are in front of them. All to better help you drive revenue.

There is no such thing as too much knowledge. Respect it, build on it and leverage it to create your success. Drive its

Growing the Business Is Where the Greatest Challenges Are

importance down through your enterprise. Make it become part of the way you do business.

"The Extra Step is Often the Difference between Real Entrepreneurial Success and Just Getting By."

We've all gotten them – a LinkedIn Connection request from someone who purports to be your friend, and you have no idea who this person is. I never accept that kind of invitation because it's just lazy (and untrue, because we're not friends). They took the time to find me but didn't go the extra step to find a reason why they wanted us to connect. So they wasted their 90% effort, not going that last 10%.

The extra step.

Examples of going the extra step are all around us. The athlete or team that works that extra thirty minutes every day on fundamentals. The sales person who's still making calls long after his or her colleagues are long gone for the day. The student who does the extra credit work in hopes that they'll make the honor society.

And it's that extra step that often defines an entrepreneur, their small business and the difference between them achieving real success and just getting by.

Growing the Business Is Where the Greatest Challenges Are

What can you do to go that extra step in your small business?

Start with your employees. Help them understand not just what they have to do but why, and in that context, how it helps both them and the company. Allow them latitude to make minor decisions without asking for permission. When they're wrong, don't take away the decision-making, but explain how they erred and help them learn from their mistakes.

With your suppliers, explain to the key ones, where they fit in the delivery of your product and service and how critical their product or service is to that delivery. In short, make them a part of that delivery. Ask them for help in trimming margins, by finding ways that they can reduce their cost to you, but trade them a guarantee of a certain level of business over time, given that they can meet the cost and schedules necessary.

And finally, for customers, show them appreciation and give them a voice. As for appreciation, don't just send them a token holiday gift once a year, but all throughout the year as they order, find special ways to thank them either through special offers or special services. They will, in turn, appreciate things that help their business more than the fruitcake or the cheese basket!

As for a voice, if you don't have one, form a user group or a customer feedback group, whose role it will be feedback, to keep your company aware of issues and opportunities with your product or service that's upfront and personal. Encourage that voice in helping you to enhance and build ever better products and services and create an even greater voice with more customers.

Go the extra step. For the entrepreneur it will truly be the difference between a thriving small business and one that is just getting by.

"Be Careful What You Wish For...Success Always Comes at a Price!"

Ask any small business owner and they will almost always tell you the same thing. If they could just grow their business bigger and faster, everything would be terrific. Not so fast, there my young business warriors! Growth and success are not the same. And further, all success comes at a price.

First, let's address the growth issue.

You always want to grow the business. But, growth for growth's sake is sometimes detrimental to the business. I would guess 75% of all of the inquiries I get from prospective clients come from companies whose "growth is stalled." Yet when I ask them where they think they should be and why, and further, why they're not there, they simply have no answers.

You should rationalize why and how you want to grow. Playing the game just to achieve "the scoreboard" (kind of like professional athletes' salaries) can create all sorts of problems for you.

You always want to grow in a measured way so you can effectively manage that growth (and have the capital to support it). Next, you want to do it, profitably. Two fairly, self-evident points. Yet, many entrepreneurs find themselves either growing too fast and not having the infrastructure or the cash flow to support that growth, or they are growing with reduced profitability or both.

Growth requires a plan. Previously, I touched on the importance of a plan, throughout the life of a business. The plan helps you rationalize growth. New products, new customers, new markets, etc. It forces you to determine the strategies and tactics you will use to achieve that growth, including what infrastructure changes you will need to achieve and support it and how you will fund it (remember my rule of thumb from previous blog posts – about 35% - 40% annual growth is about all you can expect out of cash flow, unless you have a very unique business model – they're out there, but few and far between). And, of course, it should be flexible enough for you to modify it along the way.

And now comes the even harder part. Let's say your growth plan works and you achieve the success you were after. It will come at a price!

The business will no longer be so easy to manage. You might have doubled staff, expanded your facility requirements and your payroll may have doubled or even tripled. The challenges of the early stage will seem like "child's play" compared to the growth stage. You will lament about how easy it used to be when it was only you and your three earliest employees.

And this is another crossroads for small business owners.

Growing the Business Is Where the Greatest Challenges Are

Success means that some professional management needs to be added to the organization - folks who have "been there," to assist you with further managing and growing the business. And your biggest test – to maintain and expand the culture that you have built so that the new employees embrace and thrive within it and this continues to translate to existing and new customers.

For the entrepreneur, growth and success are always challenges to reach. And, they come at price. But the price is, most often, well worth it. The price encompasses growth of a different nature – personal and professional, stretching and challenging the entrepreneur to new heights, bringing satisfaction and value way beyond just the balance sheet! It is the building and growing of a team to drive the business. You are no longer alone!

Chapter 11 – What's Your End Game? And Beyond?

"What's Your "End Game?" Do You Really Have One? Or Need One?"

Entrepreneurs start businesses for various reasons. Some because of their belief in a concept they have developed. Others because they have a desire to make an impact on society or the world. Still others because they just want to escape the corporate world and be able to control their own destiny. Or some combination of all three.

But few entrepreneurs give much thought to where their business might or should lead. Their ultimate purpose. Their "end game."

For many, it either simply evolves, or worse, they wake up one day and realize they've spent five or ten or more years with no real objective in mind, zigging and zagging from thing to thing, making some progress but toward no particular purpose.

Your "end game" should define why you are in business. It might be primarily financially driven - to develop and grow the business to a certain level, over a certain time and then sell it. Or, it might be much loftier - to create more of a societal impact, improving conditions, changing habits, addressing needs in some segment of the population or the world. Or, it might be something as simple as to create a good living for yourself, while doing work you love and

What's Your End Game? And Beyond?

delivering specialized products or services, on some small scale. It could mean a short-term, 3-5 year objective, or it could define a "lifestyle" business that ends when you decide you no longer want to do it.

Whatever it is or how you define it, it should be as specific as you can make it and it should be as personal to you (and your partners, if you have any) as possible. It should be the reason for your business' existence; why you work 60-70 hours for sub-market compensation. Why you celebrate the small victories of your staff or company. Why you can't wait to get in, in the morning, why you are the last one to leave each night.

It is simply the answer to the question every entrepreneur or small business owner asks himself/herself at multiple points in the enterprise's history – "why am I doing this?"

Know the answer. You'll still ask the question, but, at least, it will just be a reminder, rather than a deep soul-search.

And, as important, you should review your "end game," at least yearly, to continually understand if your initial "why you are doing this" still makes sense. Without it, your small business is like a "cork in the water" just bobbing along, driven by whatever the market currents happen to be.

Determine your "end game," as early in the game as possible. Continually review it to be sure it still makes sense and then chase it with every fiber of your being!

"'Take This Exit' – Selling Your Business: The Entrepreneur's Potential End Game" - Stage I – The Decision to Sell

Selling a business can be the single most important decision of an entrepreneur's life. But it's more than just making the decision. It's an emotionally charged, often deeply personal matter for you, the entrepreneur.

Your business is typically the single largest element of your asset base and estate, often with both real capital tied up and huge amounts of sweat equity invested. And it's probably been the center of your life, with relationships that have been built with partners, employees and customers that are nearly family-like. Often, it's not just a company that has been created, but also a culture. It not only has your imprint, but the blood and sweat of partners, employees and, perhaps, your own family.

But with all this at stake, few entrepreneurs ever plan their exit. Typically, they first really begin to think about it when a prospective buyer approaches them. Or worse, when external pressures, like health, family or partner problems force the issue. And even those that actually do some planning for their exit, find it can be an overwhelmingly complicated decision with layers of questions to be answered before beginning to move ahead and still more to consider once you do.

To help you better understand and organize the process, we will break it into four basic stages – The Decision, The Plan, The Approach and The Deal.

In addressing Stage I – The Decision - some critical questions are raised that should be answered to see if and when selling is right for you.

Why Do It?
Why consider selling? Have you been approached by a prospective buyer or merger partner? Are there expansion or capital issues that would be better addressed with a larger partner with deeper pockets, more infrastructure and greater reach? Does it seem time to "cash out," get your estate in order or have you simply "had enough" and want to move on? Have you taken the company as far as you believe you can, given your management capabilities? Are you intrigued by another business concept that you want to develop? Are you weary of the financial pressure or employee issues and want a "partner" to take on that burden?

In short, there should be a specific reason or reasons to sell. They could be found in answers to any one or some combination of the previous questions ...or even some other consideration such as a major conflict in a family-owned business. Simple or complicated, weighing these is a crucial first step in the process. Whatever your rationale, it is the foundation of the decision.

What Are Your Expectations from a Sale? Are They Realistic?
The question then becomes how to realistically value the business? Remember, "there are no ugly children," in the

eyes of a parent, and "beauty is in the eye of the beholder." Can you objectively arrive at a value? Have you researched selling prices of comparable businesses in your market sector are receiving? Do your expectations far exceed those current valuations, expressed as a multiple of revenue or EBITDA?

And a word of caution about valuation. It can become not unlike the dollar figure of a contract for a professional athlete – a "scoreboard" for value, the "number" you can flaunt to other members at the club or a trade group meeting. However, while acknowledging that the maximum selling price is a prime objective, this isn't just about getting a certain valuation. It's truly about what you get to actually "keep" after taxes and professional fees, regardless of how and when you are paid.

And How About After the Sale?
Whether you plan to stay on with the company or move on after a sale, there are a myriad of options for payment that can have costly tax implications. This is where advice, both professional and practical, is well worth it. Talk to professional advisors, particularly your lawyer and accountant. Talk to owners who have sold their businesses, both those who ended up happy and not so. Ask those from the investment banking community for their opinion. Consider getting a professional valuation done to get a baseline, realizing, however, that a buyer will only pay what they think the business is worth, not what a valuation claims it is.

Could You Live with the Result?
After establishing why you're selling and what you expect that sale to bring, understand the changes that typically result from a sale – some good, some... maybe, just okay.

What's Your End Game? And Beyond?

The good results are real easy to identify. No more financial or personal pressure and all that that implies – richer personal bank account; capital available for growth (if you stick around), or maybe a short consulting gig or board seat before you "ride off into the sunset" (if you don't). There could be new availability of management depth, perhaps international business expansion and an opportunity for more personal and/or professional growth (if you stick around), no more worries about benefits plans, supplier problems or off-shore price pressures (if you don't).

But how about the "just okay" results – actually the tradeoffs made for all of the positives you get?

For an entrepreneur, selling his or her company is akin to *putting your child up for adoption*. Harsh thought, perhaps, but the analogy holds. You have raised the "child" to this point and you will always be your "child's parent," but now your company will have a new "parent" that will be responsible for and control its life! There are deep emotions tied to this notion. Consider them seriously.

Plus, you won't be "king" anymore. And we all know "it's good to be king!" If you stay, you WILL have a boss – someone to whom you will have to answer! Perhaps, many new bosses. Your control over company direction and how capital is allocated will be reduced and sometimes, even minimized. And a new, different, maybe better, maybe worse, corporate culture will be introduced and you'll be center stage in front of a new and highly judgmental audience.

The unfortunate consequences of not realistically considering the potential scenarios of a post-sale situation and thinking through whether or not you can accept what it might bring cannot be emphasized enough. Most disillusionment and unhappiness that have occurred in "bad sales" happened because those entrepreneurs only considered the plusses and glossed over what they could be trading for those good things. Make no mistake; while there are sales that have worked out phenomenally well, there are always tradeoffs.

Why Sell Now?

If you understand why you want to sell and fully accepted the implications of a sale, the next thing to consider is timing. And timing IS everything!

Your company's recent operating history as well as market conditions, both overall and in your specific industry, will drive both value and the timing of the sale. Have you just come off a couple of your best years ...or your worst? Is your industry sector suddenly "hot" ...or "stone cold?" How have valuations in your industry and for comparable businesses been over the last six to twelve months? Is there some pressing need either for the business or for you personally to consider a sale now? An example would be a pending contract requiring serious capital infusion or more infrastructure, on the business side. On the personal side, divorce, children's issues, either yours or a partner's, could be driving the need to sell.

Again, answering some of these key questions will determine if the timing is right. Sometimes, there is no choice – a down market, personal pressures or health problems may force the issue. In virtually all cases, inadvertent timing will adversely affect valuation. Most buyers are fairly astute and will uncover or discern your real reasons for selling, regardless of what you tell them.

If the business is coming off a bad year or two, and there is no overriding reason to sell, consider taking the steps

What's Your End Game? And Beyond?

needed to get your numbers back to where they should be before proceeding. If the overall M&A market is soft, as it has been for the last few years, realize that there will be buyers, just fewer of them, offering lower values. If valuations in your market sector are lagging behind those of other sectors with which they've always been comparable, perhaps waiting another couple of quarter (or more) will make far better sense.

In any case, timing will be a major consideration both for the available buyers who might have an interest and the selling price you might receive. Key words of advice – it is always better to sell a little too soon...than a little too late!

Now It's Decision Time.
If there were questions you need to think more about or answers you didn't like, take the time to address each. If there are nagging doubts, or answers that raised a whole other series of difficult questions, think about those some more and either talk to or bring in the experts. If all other issues have been addressed, but the timing is wrong, for whatever reason, wait. This is a decision that not only affects you, personally and professionally, but your family and your extended family in your company.

On the other hand, if you're satisfied that you've addressed and answered all of the key questions, then the decision to proceed should be obvious. Get ready to roll up your sleeves. The real work is just beginning. Now it's getting ready for "prime time," and creating The Plan. More on this in future posts.

"'Take This Exit' – Selling Your Business: The Entrepreneur's Potential End Game" - Stage II – The Plan

Plan your exit and then execute your plan.

The process of selling a business is one that can easily get out of control. It can chew up huge amounts of your time, cause you to "take your eye off the ball," negatively affect management of day-to-day business and can often impact the very value that's been built up over the years.

A typical sale will take a minimum of six months to up to a year or more from the time you confirm your decision to sell. For these reasons, it is essential that you develop a pro-active plan and seriously consider how to best use professional advice in preparation for the sale itself.

Think Hard about Getting an Advisor
Business owners who have been most satisfied with the outcome of their sale most often have used professional advisors. Your accountant and attorney will be invaluable in helping you through the process, but they, alone, will not be enough. Successful sellers have tended to use an intermediary like an investment banker or M&A advisory firm. There are boutique firms that specialize in working

with smaller businesses. They will help you package your company, creating a summary "selling" document that will go to prospective buyers (oftentimes known as "the book"). They also effectively guide a seller through the complicated process of preparation, finding the right buyer and helping negotiate the deal.

Professional advisors will have seen situations you are now facing multiple times each year with multiple clients. Most business owners may only get to do this once…ever! Effectively using these professionals can save time, money and unnecessary aggravation, to say nothing of the effect on your quality of life during and after the transaction.

Select the one you are most comfortable with and let them lead and guide the process. The more responsibility they take on, the less impact the process will have on your day-to-day management of the business. Weigh their experience and the scope of their proposed engagement against the fees they charge. But by all means use them. This is a critical element of a successful sale, possibly the single most important financial and professional event in your life.

What Do You Need to Do to Get Ready?
At its core, selling a business is no different than selling a product. It should be presented in the best possible light, promoting its positive aspects, while downplaying those that are less than stellar. Your financial reporting, in particular, should be as "buttoned up" as possible. There should be at least three years' worth of financial reports reviewed and prepared by an outside accounting firm. Having audited statements is a real plus, but not absolutely necessary. If you have neither, you should, at least, have the previous fiscal year reviewed and prepared. Tax filings alone don't present the true picture of a business, nor will they satisfy a buyer.

If there is a business plan that describes your company's objectives and strategies for the next several years, that's also a positive, especially in helping an advisor prepare "the book." Even a rudimentary one will do. It shows prospective buyers that you are planning for growth, not just hoping it will happen. At minimum, there should be a basic plan for the current year and a forecast for at least two beyond that. A good rule of thumb for preparation is "three years back, three years forward" for presenting your company. Prospective buyers will want to know results you've had and what you're targeting, so they know what can be expected from the business.

Words of caution: don't develop a forecast that shows growth at a rate significantly higher than what you have achieved in the past. Unless there are specific and defensible growth strategies that back it up – new products, new distribution, etc., - it will erode your credibility. Further, overly optimistic projections won't impact "up front" valuation, but could be used against you, by appearing to create more future value, and an earn-out scenario that you have no chance of attaining. This will be touched on in greater depth, later.

Are There "Skeletons in Your Closet?"
Most companies know their strengths well. Few, however, readily admit to or understand their weaknesses. Every business has "warts." Some have more than others. Some have bigger ones than others. No matter, the prospective buyer will find each one ...sooner or later. Recognizing what the "warts" are and being prepared to discuss why they exist and how they can be fixed is the most prudent course. They can't and won't be ignored.

What's Your End Game? And Beyond?

Sometimes there are more than simple "warts." There may be proverbial "skeletons in the closet." For instance is there some major issue that may have occurred in years past, that has since been corrected? Examples would be a major customer or employee problem, or an issue that has yet to be resolved, such as a lawsuit, an expiring patent or a defect in a product that triggered warranty issues.

In any event, it is better to be prepared to tell a prospective buyer about these problems early in the process rather than have them discovered later in the due diligence process as you move closer toward closing. While it may turn away some buyers, it's better than having a buyer uncover problems somewhere down the line, then either substantially reduce the amount of their offer, or far worse, angrily walk away from the deal on the table, questioning your integrity. And after having expended a lot of time, energy and expense getting there.

There's at least one buyer out there who will buy the business, "warts and all." They should learn of all known problems and not have to dig them out! Be ready to show and tell them, whether they ask or not.

What Are You Looking for from Any Deal?
In the Decision Stage, we reviewed the necessity for realistic expectations. Now is the time to frame out how you would like to see those expectations tied into the needs and requirements you have for any transaction to be truly acceptable. Monetary and non-monetary; both are equally important.

Clearly, how payment is made varies with virtually every deal. You may have certain financial needs and requirements that are paramount: a certain amount of cash in the bank, a retirement fund, children's college fund, your estate, etc. Or there may be simply cash flow needs on a monthly, quarterly or yearly basis. Then there may be certain perks that you expect to continue for the foreseeable future.

Each of these issues will be flavored by whether you leave the company some time shortly after the closing, or you stay on for a considerable period of time. And don't worry about structure. Deal structure will be somewhat dictated by whom the buyer is and how they prefer to do transactions. Determine what's acceptable, and when you expect it, since not all monetary compensation may be paid at closing.

In the non-monetary area (even though some items may carry some form of remuneration), consider that if you intend to "ride off into the sunset," how long of a transition are you willing to provide the prospective buyer? If you intend to stay, what role do you expect to be playing in your former company and for how long? And what about non-competition agreements? The buyer will ask for them whether you go or stay. What do you feel is a reasonable time period for a non-compete, once you've left the company? What about your people? Out of loyalty, are there certain people that you want to be taken care of either through employment contracts or special perks after the sale?

Again, advisors can be of great help here. They've been through this dozens of times and they can counsel as to what is reasonable and what may not be and what any tax ramifications there may be.

The Buyer – Strategic vs. Financial
A word here on "strategic" vs. a "financial" buyer. A strategic buyer is one where the combination with your company has implications beyond simply combining income

statements and balance sheets. Beyond revenue, profits or assets, they bring something to the table (often capital or other resources) and you bring something to the table (often a product or a market that they see multiple expansion capability). Of course, the combination has to make financial sense, but are really looking more at the big picture.

A financial buyer is simply looking at the numbers and how the transaction can be accretive to their earnings. In most instances, valuations are much higher with strategic buyers than with financial ones.

The Buyer – Who's the "Right One" for You?
If you have already been approached by a buyer with whom you are comfortable, then you may very well have the "right" buyer. However, if a buyer is not on your doorstep, where and how you find the "right" buyer, the one who'll not only give you the "right" price and present the "right" opportunity for you and your employees, is really based on what kind of company you're looking to partner with. You need to create a profile of what that "right" buyer might look like.

This is a completely subjective judgment, dependent on your specific situation and specific requirements. For example, getting the maximum price is always a major objective. If that is the only objective then a strategic buyer, one from your own or a closely associated industry sector, might be targeted for the best fit.

For some entrepreneurs, continuation of the business at its current location with its current employees staying in place, and an ongoing advisory role for the entrepreneur may be an overriding objective. Then the ideal buyer might be former operating manager, with access to capital, who is looking for a business to run, or a private equity fund (but know that this will be a financial buyer). In any event, it is paramount to understand what you want to accomplish in a sale. Revisit the Why question we talked about in Stage I.

To help profile the "right" buyer, try to establish some criteria for judging prospective buyers. For example,

- <u>Corporate structure of buyer</u> – Would you prefer that the buyer be a public company, private company, or an individual/investor group?

- <u>Type of buyer</u> - Should the buyer be a strategic buyer, who might value your business in an aggressive way, but who might shut down a good part of your operation due to redundancy with theirs? Or a financial buyer, who might not give you optimum valuation but would want to keep you and your operation intact?

- <u>Size of buyer</u> – What revenue range should the buyer be in? This is really a comfortability issue. Do you want to be part of a multi-billion dollar company, a smaller company that's a market leader or a company that's similar in size to yours (sort of a merger of equals)?

- <u>Location of buyer</u> – Should the buyer be a domestic or international company? Perhaps, one of the reasons to sell is the inability to tap a burgeoning international market. Or east coast versus west coast?

Whatever criteria you establish for profiling prospective buyers, keep them simple and relevant to what's important to you. Clearly, any buyer must have the resources to meet your price. There will be other considerations, chief among them, the corporate "culture" that your company would be

What's Your End Game? And Beyond?

entering. Those issues will be explored as the approach is developed for prospective buyers.

"'Take This Exit' – Selling Your Business: The Entrepreneur's Potential End Game" - Stage III – The Approach

Now that you've made your decision to sell and developed your plan to proceed, you're ready for "prime time" – finding the "right" buyer at the "right" price with the "right" deal for you. Your professional advisors will play a major role in helping you effect the transaction that will meet all critical requirements. In fact, from this point forward, you will rely more and more on them.

How Do You Find the "Right" Buyer?
If you want to sell but you haven't been approached by a buyer with whom you are comfortable, finding the "right" one is a significant challenge and takes some effort.

More often than not, that "right" buyer comes out of your industry or one that is closely associated with it. You may already have a list of potential or prospective buyers. A list of names is not enough. Obtaining deeper background information relative to the profile you established when you developed your plan is key to evaluating who that prospective "right "buyer or buyers might be. This is both difficult and time-consuming. If you haven't already gone through this process before, the data gathering should be put in the hands of an outside advisor who can assist in the reviewing and screening process.

Research is critical in understanding the prospective buyers on your target list. Obviously, review their website(s) to get a feeling for how they present their company to customers and the public at large. Don't just look at product or service descriptions, but look at the management team they've assembled, where they come from and how long they've been with the company. This will begin to tell something about their culture. Also, take the time to check out their press releases. These are clues to what's been happening with the prospective buyer's company and what management judges to be important. For example, if the press releases tend to focus only on product announcements as opposed to customer announcements, they may more focused on technology or operations than marketing.

If some of the targeted companies are public, look at recent Security and Exchange Commission filings. Check out the free Edgar site - www.sec.gov/cgi-bin/srch-edgar, which lists all reports for the last ten years: quarterly – 10Qs, annual – 10Ks and proxy statements – 14As. There's wealth of information there as well as in the 8-Ks, which describe major changes in the company such as acquisitions, change of accounting firms, equity infusions, etc. Try to determine what other companies they've acquired and how much they paid as a multiple of earnings or revenue.

From the research, you and your advisors can cull out the ones who don't fit your profile and target a group of up to a dozen potential buyers. The question becomes how do you most effectively, and confidentially (more on that later) approach them? At this stage, anonymity is paramount and again where your advisor plays a major role.

How Do You "Quietly" Engage in the Selling Process?
Since no sale is complete until "the check clears," you'll want to keep the process as quiet as possible, since it can impact employees, customers and suppliers, alike.

While you're completing your preparation work for a sale, it's going to be difficult to not have key employees know "something is up." Often, these key employees are ones you've cultivated and professionally grown over time, and are an important part of the business' value. Further, they have a stake in the company, regardless of whether they have actual equity. You don't want them to be surprised.

Whether you've been approached by another company that you consider to be a "right" buyer or are embarking on finding the "right" buyer, you're probably correct to tell these key employees, confidentially, about what's happening. This keeps them "in the loop," and can assuage their fears by describing your plan for their future roles.

A word of caution: keep the group with "the need to know" as small and as trustworthy as possible. No gossips. Nothing will bring a company to its knees faster than employee unrest over the "unknown," be it buyer or sale.
And what about customers and suppliers?

No and no! Whoever is told, the circle should be small and kept internal. Customers and suppliers can get very uncomfortable with the prospect of a sale, plus are often a direct pipeline to competitors. And you know competitors will use whatever they can to beat you. Your advisor, as a confidential "go between" providing the company with anonymity, is the most prudent way to approach any prospective buyer.

What's Your End Game? And Beyond?

How Does the Process Work?
Prospective buyers on your target list are "blindly" contacted by your advisor via letter, e-mail or telephone with a broad description of your company provided, but without specifically identifying the company by name. After follow-up, if there is interest, typically, the prospective buyer is asked to sign a confidentiality agreement and is sent a summary document (typically, an executive summary of "the book") that highlights the company's history, financial performance and forecast, products, operations and management team.

There are usually a series of follow-up telephone calls with questions and sometimes a request for more information or clarification of some of the information presented. If feelings are still positive, the next steps are, typically, sending them the full "book," and then a series of face-to-face meetings at your site and potentially at the site of the buyer. This may happen with more than one prospective buyer and it may happen in different ways, but once any face-to-face meetings take place, "chemistry" and "fit" are the determining factors as to whether "courtship" ensues.

How Do You Move the "Courtship" Along and How Will You Know It's Really "Love?"
If your business is as valuable as you think it is, at some point, there will be either one or a series of prospective buyers who will "come calling." It will be "courtship," plain and simple. If possible, multiple "courtships" should be encouraged. It will take up a little more time, but will serve as both a good comparative analysis between prospective buyers, as well as an opportunity for competitive bidding.

During "courtship" everybody will be on his or her best behavior. Expect talk of some synergistic "nirvana" the combined companies can reach through a union with yours and the prospective buyer's. Extraordinarily similar views of many things will be found, both professional and personal. Eye-popping potential purchase price ranges may be thrown around, raising unreal expectations. As in courtship - keep your head and don't get swept off your feet! Understand and learn as much as you can about your prospective partner. Review the earlier research. Ask hard questions. For example, if you have a unique employee benefit, ask if they have anything similar for their employees. Does their management style correspond with or conflict with your own? What is their strategic direction? How do they see your company contributing to that strategy?

Get to know some of the key executive management people on a personal level. What kind of personal values do they appear to have? Those will spill over into and/or frame their professional values. Moreover, their corporate culture should be represented by those values. How do you feel yours will blend with theirs? How do they see the two companies working together? Besides price, it is the single, most important element of any successful transaction.

To further understand culture, when you visit their offices, talk to their staff while there. Judge whether the people actually enjoy working there, or are putting on a good show for you. If they've done acquisitions in the past, talk to prior sellers, particular those no longer with the company. Find out why they might have left. Your advisors should accompany you to any meetings or visits. They'll give you a more objective opinion, with less-biased observations.

At the same time, provide the prospective buyer with as much information as you judge to be reasonable. Financial reports, and product literature are reasonable. A prospective buyer asking to conduct full-blown due

What's Your End Game? And Beyond?

diligence before making an offer is not. Remember, this is "courtship." Due diligence before "expressing true love" (a real offer) is not unlike asking to grill family members and reviewing bank statements while you're simply dating. And don't be pressured into naming your price to a buyer. It's a sure way to get less.

Let them tell you! Once you've put a number out there, it will only go down! **Yoda's First Law of Negotiation** -"He who mentions a number first…loses!"

The long and the short of it is that the relationship with the prospective buyer must "feel right." It's too important to you and your staff for it not to. They will have "warts" also. And theirs won't get better, either. Be sure you can live with the "intended's," warts and all, regardless of what the final offer might be.

How Do You Get the Best Proposal from the Right Buyer…in the Shortest Time?
Once it looks like a match, both in terms of what they're telling you about their "ballpark" price and what you're feeling about the kind of company and people they are, it's time for a deal to come together. Most important: stay out of direct negotiations, if at all possible. Designate one of your advisors (the one with the most experience) to work with the prospective buyers in framing a deal. In negotiations over deal terms, sellers can't be objective and are likely to be emotional - remember the "child up for adoption" analogy from the Decision Stage. In most situations you'll be overmatched. Your counterpart will either be an executive who's negotiated dozens of these deals over the last several years or a professional, hired for the situation, also with significant experience. That kind of firepower should be working on your behalf as well.

There will certainly be some preliminary discussions that outline what the prospective buyer is thinking about in terms of deal price and structure. Based on those general discussions, define with your advisors basic parameters of what you're looking for and then give them some room to negotiate. Preliminary review with your tax advisors is important, to ensure that the structure and payment terms provide optimum tax benefit, allowing you to "keep" as much as possible.

A prospective buyer will want to delay making a specific offer as long as possible so they can continue gathering more information about you and your company. They will continue to press you for a price. A buyer wants to try to pay as little as possible and is looking for every edge. Don't take it personally, that just the way it works.

Once it appears that there is genuine interest and serious discussions about terms have occurred, have your advisors push the buyer to commit an offer to paper as early as possible, with sufficient time for you to review it and react. If there is more than one interested party, clearly that will drive price. Here's really where your advisors earn their money, by keeping as many interested parties at the table for as long as possible. An "auction" is good!

An offer will most likely take the form of a non-binding letter of intent or term sheet. Either should succinctly describe all of the key business deal points. This would include post transaction items like employment contracts or consulting agreements, but might only describe remuneration and term, rather than the specific details. Nothing major should be left "for later."

Words of caution about an offer. Wherever possible, get as much of the total transaction value as early as possible. The

What's Your End Game? And Beyond?

later the payments, the less likely they will occur, unless they are guaranteed in some way. Generally, it's not because the buyer will renege, but more because those later payments are usually based on some future milestone being met. Shy away from "earn-outs," if at all possible. If much of your company's value is still in the future and an earn-out necessary, keep it simple and try to base it on top-line revenue. This avoids haggling about how various costs are treated or assigned to arrive at some profit number basis.

Typically, an iteration or two will be needed to get the deal points to where everybody's comfortable. Then, there are terms to which both parties agree, can execute and from which a definitive purchase agreement can be created. However, due diligence discoveries, lawyers from both sides, and time itself can make the deal go away. All three can work against completing a sale unless they have been anticipated and addressed in advance.

Now comes the hard part – getting the deal done!

"'Take This Exit' – Selling Your Business: The Entrepreneur's Potential End Game" - Stage IV – The Deal

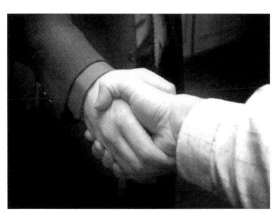

Unfortunately, signing a letter of intent does not a deal make. The document merely puts down on paper the agreement in principle between you and the buyer. Typically, a letter of intent is non-binding, since the buyer has yet to conduct due diligence to verify that everything that the offer was based on is as you've described...or as the buyer understood. These are, often, two different perceptions.

While the Approach stage can be analogous to courtship, the Deal stage is like the engagement period and planning for the wedding, rolled up into one. It's when you both really get to know each other and all the "warts" are more closely examined. Further, it's when your employees have to be briefed about what may happen with the company and what it may mean to them, personally and professionally.

It can also be a very stressful period with the seemingly endless demands on your time. Preparing for and living through due diligence can be disruptive. There may be legal hurdles. And through it all, the business must continue to run. If a seller is aware of the potential "hazards," they can be anticipated, dealt with and the outcome can still be the "right" deal.

What Do You Tell Your Staff and How Do You Keep Them Focused?

Once there is a signed the letter of intent and the buyer presents their due diligence plans, the potential sale can no longer be kept within your inner circle. Since the buyer will almost assuredly have people on site, there is almost no choice but to disclose plans to employees. But what is said and how it is said will impact how well fears are allayed and employees' focus will be kept on carrying out day-to-day responsibilities.

Employees should be told there is an offer leading to a possible sale. No need to go into how it came about. It should be treated as a positive reflection on the company. Clearly, if some or all employees are shareholders, a sale can be very positive, with potential cash in their pockets. On the other hand, fears are going to arise regarding change and job security. If specific requirements have been given to the buyer regarding staff and operations, discussing those with the employees will reinforce their importance if the deal is to be successful.

In no case should employees be told anything other than what has been explicitly agreed to with the buyer, particularly conditions that are still under negotiation. Explain that what is on the table is an offer, not a deal…yet. Frame for them the process ahead. Managing employee expectations is in everyone's best interest. If a deal does not happen, all will need to continue working together, keeping the company successful.

How Do You Make Due Diligence Work for You Instead of Against You?
Due diligence is the process that is used to verify data gathered about the company. Buyers use it to better understand the company's operations, finances and legal obligations. Typically this includes reviewing accounting and personnel practices, internal systems and policies, operational processes, contracts, backlog and sales forecasting, to name just a few. Your staff will be heavily involved. Customers may be interviewed, usually anonymously. Be aware that some buyers also use due diligence findings as a justification to reduce their offer.
Make due diligence an ally.

First, have the buyer provide a list of all data that they will need before the process begins. Next, prepare two binders with copies of all requested information: one for your files, one for theirs. Assign a work area, preferably a conference room or vacant office where the buyer's due diligence team can be housed while they're reviewing data and conducting interviews. Assign a "point person" from your organization, preferably senior management, to coordinate the effort with the buyer's organization. Brief any staff member who might need to interact with the buyer's due diligence team. Prepare everyone, covering what they might be asked and that they should respond honestly.

How Do You Avoid Surprises?
If you've identified "warts," or even some "skeletons," prepare to discuss them in some detail and have a "fix plan" ready, if possible. If there have been "skeletons" in the history of the company, that may or may not surface during due diligence, take the prudent path and readily offer to describe each, including their disposition, to the buyer's team.

What's Your End Game? And Beyond?

If the buyer uncovers something unexpected during the process, perhaps something judged to have been unimportant or simply not mentioned previously, be as forthcoming with information and answers as possible. Defensiveness during due diligence is a natural reaction, although a red flag to buyers. Keeping cool under fire is critical for both you and your staff.

Are There "Skeletons in the Buyer's Closet" – How Do You Conduct Due Diligence on Your Prospective Partner?
As the old saying goes, "what's good for the goose is good for the gander." Unfortunately, few sellers do in-depth due diligence on the buyer. No law against it, it's just that the buyer is the one committing the capital, and is usually better prepared. Most buyers have either done an acquisition before or are being advised by seasoned professionals who have.

However, you the seller also have much at stake, having spent a good deal of your working life devoted to this business, with most of your assets tied up in it. Isn't it wiser to, at least, know more than you uncovered in your initial research and in some of the "courtship" meetings? Are you able to objectively assess your prospective partner?

Here's another context in which it is best to use professional advisors. They will have had significant experience with both buyers and sellers. Together, draw up an equivalent list of data to be reviewed and questions to be answered by the buyer. While it may be an unusual request, it will prove its value as the process moves forward. Information gathered will help objectively clarify the buyer's plans, culture, how they operate and how these compare with your own enterprise. This exercise will lead to a better understanding of real synergies versus ones expressed during courtship. Above all, a seller must answer the key question – how WILL we operate AFTER the deal?

Clearly, if the buyer is part of a larger company, focus on the buyer's organization and gain some insight into its parent, but only as it relates to the buyer's operation, since you'll be in the same chain of command.

If the buyer has no problem with your team conducting due diligence, that speaks to confidence in who they are and how they've represented themselves. On the other hand, if they limit what you can know or ask, some "red flags" are being raised. If they turn you down completely, it may be time to re-think who your partner is and if this marriage can really work.

Don't Spend the Money Yet - How Do You Make Sure the Deal They Offered Is the Deal You Finally Get?
The biggest mistake an entrepreneur can make in the process of selling his or her business is "spending the money" before the deal is done! This is not meant literally, but figuratively. That is, the seller begins to focus on either the deal or "the money," and the positive changes those will bring to his or her life and company, long before the deal is finalized. Far worse is that in a majority of transactions, the deal that is initially agreed to in the letter of intent, changes significantly by the time it gets to the definitive agreement. Most often, they are the result of "surprises" uncovered in due diligence.

Once sellers begin to think of the deal as done before it is, they weaken their bargaining position, wanting the deal to happen, no matter what. And this occurs far more frequently than it should. This sometimes causes the seller to "cave in" on negotiating critical operational issues or even agreeing to changes in payment terms, in their haste to close the deal.

What's Your End Game? And Beyond?

Ensuring that the deal that they offer becomes the final deal is to have the buyer's offer based on knowing and understanding the seller's "warts" or "skeletons" ahead of time, and for the seller to maintain the attitude of "business as usual" until the deal actually closes. That is, continue to operate the company and your personal life as if there was no deal.

Further, don't allow any element of the deal you consider important left to be negotiated after the transaction is closed. Either in the zeal to get the deal done or because they will be in a stronger negotiating position once the contract is executed, the buyer may suggest a delay in the specifics such as how the companies will actually be integrated and operate, reporting structures or how bonuses will be determined, until after closing. If it's important, it should be negotiated and documented…before closing.

Finally, any negotiations that deviate from the letter of intent to the ultimate definitive agreement should only be negotiated through professional advisors. This includes employment or consulting agreements. Sellers can be too emotional with so much at stake. Plus, negotiations could be with your future boss. Serious disagreements, which can and do occur, could jeopardize your post-deal relationship.

Professional advisors, on the other hand, can wear "a black hat" and be tough negotiators representing their client's interests. Once the deal is done, they're gone. If the "hired guns" upset the buyer or his people, it will be irrelevant. You will have gotten what you wanted and won't be tainted by the process.

Can You Live with the Result? – Re-Visiting an Earlier Question Before Signing on the Dotted Line and Preventing "Seller's Remorse" Afterward.

As the process wends its way toward conclusion and the ultimate definitive agreement, it is time to conduct one more honest personal analysis of the potential deal - what it will mean to you, your future role and the role and position of the company you created.

Go back to Stage I and review the questions in the section. Can you live with the result?

There's been a lot more time to think about why sell. As a result of due diligence, there are now a lot more facts about your future partners, their plans, their operations, their people and their culture. How comfortable are you about how the two companies really fit? And how are you going to accept not being "king?" It's most likely to be a very emotional decision. At the end of the day, it has to "feel right."

Even if it turns out that it just doesn't "feel right," or you just aren't ready, you may have lost some time and spent some money, but you're still in control of your major asset until the time or the circumstance is right.

Words of caution on the definitive agreement: don't allow the legal process of "papering the deal" to get out of control. It can't be allowed to scuttle a good deal.

Counsels for each side will be trying to protect their respective client. The buyer's counsel will want to craft an agreement that is heavily weighted toward protecting the buyer and reducing buyer exposure. Seller's counsel will want an agreement that is heavily weighted toward providing the seller with the best payment terms and least onerous representations and warranties. The buyer's counsel will almost always win. The buyer is making the money commitment. Your counsel's main responsibility is to ensure that the business terms that have been negotiated have been properly described with the proper protections for you. In short, if you want the deal to happen, so must your attorney.

Finally, expect that some portion of your front-end payment, probably anywhere from 5%-20% to be held in escrow for some period of time, probably anywhere from 90 days to one year. Don't take this personally. This will be how the buyer protects himself from any representation or warranty that you've made about issues such as receivables, taxes or legal obligations. Keeping escrow to a minimum is how your counsel earns his money!

Post Close – A Brave New World, Or - How's Your New Job and Do You Like Your New Boss?

It's done. The deal's is signed, the check has cleared and you and your partner walk off into the sunset, arms intertwined, living happily ever after. Well, mostly. As in all marriages, there are bound to be compromises.

You made your money, so no more financial worries. You have, in hand, the potential security of an employment or consulting agreement and the availability of capital for your company to grow. The buyer now has a solid revenue stream, good cash flow, a strategic set of products, cross selling opportunities, more intellectual property or entry into a key market, previously impenetrable.

However, along the way, someone else came in to control of your destiny. Control was traded for liquidity and financial security. There are different and new responsibilities. Now, there's a boss, maybe for the first time ever.

Once the deal is closed, the buyer needs a return on his investment. The revenue and profit numbers signed up for have to be met. The buyer traded capital to leapfrog in either size or market by taking on a more nimble, profitable operation.

While many acquisitions have problems post-closing, many can and do work.

While there will be "bumps in the road," as in a marriage, a successful relationship needs ongoing commitment and communication from both sides. In many deals that go sideways, either buyer or seller has forgotten the initial rationale behind the combination. The rationale was based on both parties making tradeoffs. The buyer's bureaucracy may be troubling but can be worked with. It evolved before you happened on the scene. Your operation's risk-taking style could trouble the buyer. But that was what they liked about the company before the deal. The seller remembers only the good of "running the shop," glossing over or forgetting about the pressures of making payrolls and dealing with the tax authorities or bankers. The buyer is likely to recall that before the acquisition they had their own plan to enter the market that you had successfully penetrated.

In the end, the success of the business relationship will be directly related to both sides' ability to accept that the sale has effected changes to each of their operations. How well both plan for and accept those changes, allow time for the cultures to find common ground and implement reasonable integration efforts will be the key elements for that success. Then it will become a "win, win" for both the buyer and the seller.

Conclusion
As initially noted, selling a business can be the single most important decision of an entrepreneur's life. It's highly

What's Your End Game? And Beyond?

emotional, often deeply personal. The entrepreneur's business is not just a major asset of his or her life, but often the center, with relationships that have been built with partners, employees and customers that are nearly family-like. With so much at stake, it is critical that you, the entrepreneur understand the need to plan your exit. Beyond the emotions, it is a complex, time-consuming task fraught with many pitfalls.

This four-stage process should provide a framework for understanding what's involved in planning your exit and executing your plan. It should be a guide for helping prospective sellers better understand why and when to sell, what's involved in getting ready to do so and then the critical questions and steps for getting off the business ownership highway at the "right" exit.

But you'll be back. Once entrepreneurship is in your blood, you're hooked! See you soon with the next great business model!

Secrets to Entrepreneurial Success

About the Author

Lonnie L. Sciambi, "The Entrepreneur's Yoda," is Managing Director and CEO of Small Business Force, LLC. Entrepreneurs need every edge they can get to start and grow a business. Lonnie provides that edge with solutions to key issues entrepreneurs face every day. His "on the money" advice helps owners gain the returns they seek.

Whether seeking mentoring, strategic alternatives for growth or under-performing operations, strategic exit guidance or just a valuable blog post, he brings a unique viewpoint to help entrepreneurs and small business owners avoid many of the pitfalls that they, invariably, face along the way.

Lonnie's advice is long on candor, short on catchy buzzwords. No theories, no "rah-rah, feel goods!" Just practical advice for entrepreneurs and small business owners that can contribute to their success

He has been a "serial CEO," with more than thirty years' experience as a CEO of both public and private companies, across multiple industry markets. Lonnie also has some large company experience earlier in his career that includes senior management positions with EDS and Citicorp.

As an entrepreneur, he founded, grew and sold two of his own companies (although he did start several others – so he understands both success...and failure) and helped more than fifty companies establish their strategic direction and develop capital-generating business plans as advisor and mentor and invested in more than a dozen (some successfully, some not so). Lonnie also has a lot of experience fixing "broken" companies, having completed a series of successful turnarounds for eight small companies (all under $25 million) in disparate markets.

He also been involved in raising more than $350 million in capital, as an investment banker and senior executive, and had primary responsibility for nearly forty merger and acquisition transactions, more a dozen of those, entrepreneurial exits.

Lonnie began his career with IBM (to whom he is forever grateful for showing him what a real corporate culture can be, even in a large company). He received a bachelor of science degree in electrical engineering from Drexel University (to whom he's equally grateful for their co-op program that helped him "fly out of the chute").

He resides in Port Monmouth, NJ with his wife Helen and has three children, the "start-ups" of which he is most proud - Jon who lives in New York City, Sara, who lives in Miami Beach, FL and Ben, who lives in New Jersey.